Mississippi Milkwater

Mississippi Milkwater

A Memoir

Sybil Pittman Estess

ALAMO BAY PRESS
SEADRIFT•AUSTIN

Cover Art: Sybil Pittman Estess
Photos: Sybil Pittman Estess
Book Design: ABP

For orders and information:
Alamo Bay Press
Pamela Booton, Director
825 W 11th Ste 114
Austin, Texas 78701
pam@alamobaypress.com
www.alamobaypress.com

Library of Congress Control Number: 2020950515
ISBN: 978-1-943306-20-6

For my husband,

Ted L. Estess

and my sister,

Jo Cheryl Pittman Roemmele

Mississippi Milkwater

Mississippi Milkwater

Introduction

I am Sybil Arlene Pittman Estess, born November, 1942,
and raised in and around Hattiesburg, then Poplarville, Mississippi. The stories in this book provide pictures of my early life growing up in the American South prior to the Civil Rights Movement. They relate events, in the main, as I remember them.

Much has been written and argued about the differences between fiction and nonfiction. I wrote this manuscript as nonfiction, although most of the names have been changed. In these stories, I am "Samantha" or "Sam."

When my sister and I were children, if Mother didn't have enough milk for supper, she sometimes announced that we had a special treat to drink that night. She filled two glasses halfway with water, and the other half with milk, and called it "milkwater." Sometimes, we even had ice in the glass. If we wished, we could have a teaspoon of sugar and some vanilla flavoring.

Of course, the liquid was only half nourishing, and I didn't like it. But I drank it, because Mother said to, and I knew it was all that she had. My mother grew up in a family of six children without much money, and I imagine her family had plenty of "milkwaters" and other substitutes to eat or drink.

I will always have a nostalgic fondness for Mississippi as the place where I grew up, that helped forge the woman, wife, scholar, poet, mother, and teacher I became. It was also a time, however, when racial prejudice was so commonplace that it shaped my thoughts into adulthood, until education and maturity forced me to question the reasons that such hatred and injustice exist.

As I grow older, I realize my memories are shared by many who lived during this time. My hope is that this book will help keep these stories alive, providing not the names and dates of a history text, but the situated perspectives and experiences of one person who lived through it. May it serve as a reminder of that time and place, and of the fissures we are still struggling to heal.

Sybil Pittman Estess

Mississippi Album

Ben gets his draft notice: 1944

California wedding: Age three

Paternal grandparents with my father, c. 1918

Christmas with Terri Lee dolls, c. 1950

Miriam's mother's family

Part One
Jasper County

Alone in Jasper County with Lola

Mama told me to run home if I ever seen a big cloud. To not even tell the teacher – just run. I seen a big white cloud come. It was in April, I think. Mama says a big cloud meant a tornado might be a-comin'. I'm in second grade, and I'm the smartest. I have on my overalls. I don't have shoes in spring and summer. I have my tin bucket with a sweet potato and a biscuit with molasses on it. I grabbed it. I kicked up my heels and ran the three miles I walked that morning at six o'clock, when Mama makes us leave the house a-walkin' for the schoolhouse. That day I got home in the sunshine. Mama said it weren't even gonna rain that day.

Ben Cook

Lola, Samantha's daddy's mother and her grandmother in Jasper County, ate fried chicken feet, picked up a rattlesnake with her bare hands in her corn rib, popped off its head, and hid under her eating table when someone knocked at the door. And she jumped in a ditch when the first automobile was about to pass her on her dirt road with no gravel. Someone had told her that a car had gasoline in it and would blow up. Her name was Lola Morgan Cook. Her husband, Ponce de

Leon Cook, died when Sam was three years old. Her mother said Samantha was very fond of him and would hold onto his pinkie with her whole little hand while he walked her around the farm. Sam's mother thought she would never forget him. But she did.

Lola was an anxious woman just past fifty years old. She wore gingham dresses made from feed sacks and wore black, clunky, lace-up shoes. "Papa Lynn's" presence lingered in the house and on the small farm that surrounded it, especially since Mamaw Lola made frequent references to him and to how she missed and needed him.

Sam's paternal grandmother was born in 1898, the fourth of six children born to Emma Thigpen and Benjamin Morgan. Their ancestors had undergone hardships of peasant life in their English homeland and again after they migrated to America. They apparently landed in the U.S. in New York, though not at Ellis Island, not in the Virginia and North Carolina ports as many other immigrants.

Sam's ancestors eventually came south and west over the Appalachian Mountains on foot and in wagons. They homesteaded timberland that they cleared with the help of oxen so that they could grow cotton and corn somewhere near Waldrup in Jasper County, which was a new county when the Morgans first ploughed land there in the early years of the nineteenth century.

Jasper County was settled by whites who were agrarian people, many of whom still spoke a variant of Middle English. They were Baptists, Methodists and a few Presbyterians, but there were no Catholics, Episcopalians, or Jews.

Family stories recalled that the White settlers had encountered both Choctaw and Chickasaw Indians, but mostly Choctaws. Locals said that the Jasper County hills still contained Native American remains, such as arrowheads, pieces of pottery, and bones.

Sam's relatives had memories of visiting Indian burial grounds as children. Those graves were mysterious to the Anglos and often made them fearful. They said the spirits of the Native peoples were still there. Some still believed, during the 1940s and 1950s, that the spirits would return to "haint" them if they went to the burial grounds.

When Sam was five years old. she and her friend Marilyn went to Mamaw Lola's house together for a summer week. But the next summer, when Sam was six, her parents sent her to Jasper County alone. Samantha had visited her grandmother's backwoods home many times with her parents, but this would be the first time she'd spent a week alone with Mamaw Lola in the unpainted house where the only toilet was the outhouse on ground behind the shack with smoked meats. There was no running water or electricity.

It wasn't until the 1950s that modern amenities, like electricity and indoor plumbing, finally arrived in Lola's part of Jasper County. Sam's grandmother spent her entire life drawing water from her well just off the western-facing south side of the front "gallery" (open porch) with a bucket and drinking from gourds that were grown, dried, and fashioned by the farmers for use as drinking cups. Before electricity, the Cooks lit coal-oil lanterns just after dark. But in the summertime, anyone who stayed in Mamaw's house went to bed before sunset.

To bathe in the summer, Lola set a gray, galvanized tub out on the gallery. Cold water from the well was heated on the wood stove and poured into the tub. In winter, one bathed inside the house in front of the fireplace.

To the left of the gallery, behind the well, Lola grew her vegetable garden and apple and pear trees. At the edge of the garden and through a small field was the barn, which Grandpaw Lynn and his brother Hestus built with oak lumber cut from their land. The two families shared the barn, as well as the outhouse hidden around back, and the mailbox — halfway between the two Cooks' houses.

Uncle Hestus lived just up the hill and had a car that ran most of the time. After Papaw Lynn died, Hestus helped Lola out whenever she needed him, especially when something required the use of an automobile. At that time it was an all-day wagon trip just to reach Bay Springs, where Lola would shop only an hour or two and return home by dark. Bay Springs was the western county seat twenty miles away. Even in the early 1950s wagons were always parked on the hilly main streets. Most of Samantha's relatives didn't own cars and had never been more than twenty miles from their homes. To them, leaving Mississippi for any reason was unthinkable, like jumping off the earth. With a per capita income among the lowest in Mississippi (and therefore the United States), Jasper County was and is still a poor area, so a lack of financial resources made it unlikely that they would be able to leave even if they wished.

Lola also believed that all storms could kill her, her family, her friends, or anyone she loved. A terrible tornado did indeed destroy much of Jasper County in 1927. It took the life of the new husband of Lola's youngest sister, Patience, and swept their one-month old baby from her mother's arms. The baby girl was named Wyneeter, a misspelled variant of Juanita, which was always pronounced with a hard "errr" at the end. The 1927 storm put the baby one mile away in a field, totally unharmed. Around the fire one evening, Lola recalled the storm by saying, "I 'member when I seen that straw drive right into a post by that wind. But little Wyneeter, I declare, she weren't even hurt."

There were no modern comforts, such as a sofa or easy chair, in Lola's house. All the furniture was handmade from wood. Lola's eating table had unattached benches on two sides and no chairs except at the end. The picnic-style table was large enough to seat relatives and "hands." White hired hands, who were tenant farmers from closeby, ate with the family at breakfast and midday. Black hired hands, however, ate on the back steps, near the roaming chickens.

At Lola's, the food was always delicious. Hungry visitors devoured fried chicken and home-cured ham as they reached over each other at the table. In the yard, chickens of various varieties roamed around clucking, unknowingly awaiting their fate. Some mornings, before seven o'clock,

Sam watched Lola wring a chicken's neck, pluck it, and cut it up for frying. She'd hack the wishbone so Sam could eat a piece of special juicy breast. But to Lola, the best part was the feet. Watching from across the table, Sam couldn't get over the sight of Mamaw gnawing on a fried chicken foot.

Sharing the eating room with the eating table were a pine pie safe and an old oak ice box with real ice brought by an iceman who traveled down the road as often as he could. With only the icebox for refrigeration, Lola relied on other methods to preserve her food. She cured and stored pork in the smokehouse outside and pickled or poured vinegar over every vegetable, an English custom that Lola taught Samantha. Even as an adult, Sam loved the taste of vinegary vegetables, and once, as an adult living in England, she heard that the briny habit was adopted during the Middle Ages to kill germs.

Beyond these every-day foods, Mamaw loved to spoil Sam with what she considered "treats." She baked teacakes for Sam, and she promised to buy from the traveling man the red or purple syrup to make "swaate drink," a kind of Kool-Aid made from sugar syrup and red or purple dye.

Despite the teacakes and swaate drinks from Mamaw, Sam felt homesick in Jasper County, especially during the dark nights. She missed her parents and her sister Lilah Jo. She lay alone in her bed as daylight merged with dusky evening. The summer nights were warm, but when Lola went to bed at seven o'clock, she wrapped her head in a white rag, as was the custom during the colder months. She'd given Samantha a battery radio to keep her company and told her to try to tune in a Laurel station, thirty miles away through the thick woods. Sam shook the radio and fiddled with the buttons, twisting and turning. but all she heard was static. She switched the radio off and listened to the sounds of Lola's snoring accompanied by the reverberation of crickets chirping just outside her window.

Sam finally laid her head on the pillow, trying to sleep, but all she could think about was the long chicken snake Lola once found winding its way through the dresser drawers in the room where Sam slept. Lola killed that one easily, but Sam worried that there might be another one.

If Sam needed to relieve herself, she had to use the pot in her bedroom, and empty it outside the next morning. The outhouse was far down a path where she might encounter rattlesnakes. Killing rattlesnakes in the middle of the night was not an activity anyone should attempt. Mamaw had recently killed one with her bare hands in the corn crib near the overgrown pathway. One day when Sam was at her house Lola said she saw another one slithering through the grass and up into the corn crib. She screamed for Sam to bring her a hoe. Lola hacked off its head, then threw both parts of the body out of the corn crib toward Sam, who screamed and ran.

If Sam thought the first summer with Lola was frightening, worse was coming her way the following year. Her parents sent her to spend another week in Jasper County. That summer, Sam's Uncle Elton was building a house on land just down the road. Uncle Elton had inherited the land from his mother, Mamaw Lola. Uncle Elton was Ben's little brother, the second and last of Lola's children. Elton and Ben never got along well, and Ben avoided his brother as much as possible. According to family stories, Elton was jealous of Ben for being their mother's favorite.

One afternoon, Sam walked up to Elton's house in her summer dress. She liked the feel of the dusty road against her bare feet. She stood next to her father's cousin Leon and watched as the men dug the well and the water began to rise down below. The men had reached the water table. Leon was the youngest son of Patience. He had epilepsy and later died at the age of thirty-five, perhaps in part because he never took the proper medication to control his seizures. Sam and Leon watched as the hole next to Elton's house grew deeper.

Once water began to seep up, the men snagged Leon with a rope and lowered the poor, epileptic fellow to the bottom of the well. Sam stood aghast as Leon had an epileptic fit, a grand-mal seizure. The men removed the rope ladder that would have allowed him to escape and stood at the top of the well, laughing. Of course Leon was probably scared that he was going to drown.

"Look at his mouth foam," one laughed.

"And his teeth are clattering," bellowed another.

"See how his eyes go back in his head?"

"Hey, Leon! How is it down thar? How is you?"

"We better git down there and hold down his tongue with somethin'. They say they will swaller their tongue," another man said.

Samantha thought Leon would soon be covered with rising water and drown. None of the men seemed to care much that the water was rising around Leon, even though he was foaming at the mouth. No one cared either that a seven-year-old girl watched, frozen with fear.

Samantha never knew how Leon got out or how he recovered, because she ran back to Mamaw Lola's house. She ran as far and as fast as she could to get away from that, strange, evil place. She told Lola what she had seen. Her grandmother said, "There ain't nuthin I kin do."

For Mamaw Lola, who thought laughing and idleness were sins, Monday was always washday. She washed her clothes across the road from the house in the shade of a huge oak tree. That Monday, as she had done every week of her adult life, even in the worst of the summer heat, Lola built a fire under her black wash pot. As was her custom in the summer, Lola was barefoot.

Sam watched Mamaw lean over the boiling pot, stirring the clothes with a stick. She imagined her grandmother was a witch as in the fairytales her mother read to her at home in Hattiesburg. But as Sam envisioned the witch at her cauldron, Lola screamed and fell to the ground. She had stepped into the coals surrounding the wash pot. As Sam's country grandmother lay screaming in the hot dirt, one foot scorched, red, and blistered, her anguished burned into Sam's mind. Even seventy years later, sometimes when Sam closes her eyes, she can hear Lola scream, "Oh! Oh! Run,

Sam! Get hep! Run!"

But Mamaw Lola didn't say where to run. Sam looked up the hill toward Uncle Hestus's car, but it wasn't there, so she ran the other way: north. Her seven-year-old bare feet carried her as fast as she could run in the other direction toward the house of Lola's sister Lottie.

Somehow, somewhere, someone helped. Sam's memory blanked out. She had no recall of where she ended up or who used what telephone. The next thing she remembered, she was in the car with her father and mother on their way to Hattiesburg. She didn't know who kept her in Jasper County until they arrived. She didn't remember returning to Lola's house to pack her clothes, nor did she know how her grandmother arrived at the Laurel Hospital, thirty miles away.

During that summer of her seventh year, Sam still didn't know her grandmother very well. All she knew was that Mamaw Lola may have been dying from her burns.

Lola's wounds were third degree burns that never healed during the remaining two years of her life. Once, after Lola developed gangrene in that foot, the doctors threatened to amputate it. They never did, but they might have followed through if Lola had lived much longer.

No one mentioned the incident to Sam again, and no one commended her for having secured help for Mamaw.

Grief Comes to Jasper County

*My husband, Leon, grows cotton he trades at the store.
Thirty acres of what we own are fields. Eight more are
woods with a creek. Then there's my garden and my
pea patch. At four I rise and kill three chickens. I wring
their necks, pluck them, and fry them for breakfast on
the woodstove for the hands to eat with the biscuits and
ham that I cook. We heard thunder way down toward
the far field. But ain't no rain come, so we don't have
to go to the pit. It's summer now, but I still wrap my
head when I sleep.*

Lola Morgan Cook

Sam's grandfather died from a stroke at the age of fifty-three. Samantha doesn't remember Grandpa Leon, but
"Papaw Lynn," as Miriam told her many times, adored her,
and she him. Sam was three at the time. Before that, when
Sam was a toddler, she sat in Papaw Lynn's lap, put white
powder on his bald head, combed his thin hair, and said,
"There, Papaw, that good."

Papaw led Samantha by the hand around the grassless,
broom-swept yard, holding his pinkie with hers. The grand-

father-granddaughter duo strolled around the farm, visiting chickens and dogs and pigs.

A reminder of that time in Sam's life was captured and saved in a photograph of Sam on a tall mare in the Jasper County winter. In the black-and-white photograph, two-year-old Samantha is smiling, her head wrapped against the cold in a white rag. According to Miriam, Sam began screaming as the horse was led around the yard. Miriam had warned Ben's family that Sam scared easily, but they insisted she be initiated into country life.

Later that day, Sam contracted a fever of 104 degrees, which Miriam attributed to fear. In the middle of the Mississippi winter, and despite her mother's protests, they put iced rags over Sam's body to cool her down. To Miriam, the episode was further proof of the general backwardness of Jasper County.

Winter nights at Mamaw's house were particularly difficult. After the fireplace went out, they had to pile on six or more cotton quilts to keep warm. While the sheets were rough, multi-patterned and hand-sewn from feed sacks, the quilts were an act of love. Lola worked painstakingly to make each one by hand. Sometimes, though, it was so cold that even with a rag on her head and Lola's quilts to keep her warm, Sam could still see her breath in the air.

Miriam thought it was downright primitive that women had to "wrap their heads from the cold," as Mamaw Lola put it. Sam had white rags wrapped around her head often throughout her childhood whenever she was in Jasper County, even in the summer.

Lola didn't have knitted caps, which explained why she used rags to wrap her head. In fact, Mamaw Lola only owned two hats, a black felt one for winter and a yellow straw one for summer. She wore these only to Enon Baptist Church, where she and Papw traveled every Sunday in their horse-drawn wagon.

While Lola wasn't a Southern "lady," she still bowed to Jasper's gender rules. After supper during the winter, the men sat around the fireplace, roasting peanuts and sweet potatoes. There was no radio, so they talked during their leisure time. That was the only form of evening entertainment. They drank coffee from saucers, blowing on it to cool it quickly. Women never drank alcohol, but at night the men often passed around contraband moonshine, or "white lightnin'," each taking a swig from the jug. The homemade liquor was made in a still in the woods. The bottles were wrapped in paper and kept hidden in an out-of-the-way closet or cabinet.

Alcohol may have been off limits for women, but tobacco was not. Most of the men smoked corncob pipes or chewed tobacco, spitting the juice into a coffee can, while the women dipped snuff and did the same. Mamaw Lola adored her snuff so much that even when she was semi-conscious from a stroke and dying at the age of fifty-two, she begged for her snuff, which the hospital staff forbade her from having.

Another early Jasper County memory was captured in a photo of Samantha around age four, standing tall and stretching, so she could hold up a long line of fish that were caught overnight. The wintertime shot showed Samantha wearing pastel-colored overalls with the staple white rag around her head. The family put out trotlines to catch catfish along the Luak Fluppa Creek, fed by the Tallahala River and named by the Chickasaws, an indigenous tribe in the southeastern part of the U.S. No one could see the creek from Mamaw's porch, but in the summer it was always on their minds, while everyone told fishing stories. Sam loved walking with her dad down to the creek to see what was snagged on the

When Samantha grew into an older woman, her memories of Jasper County remained vivid in her mind. She still remembers it all, every image in her mind tinged with a mysterious and fearful glow. There's Lola's house, starkly unpainted, the constantly dusty road, and, farther south, at the end of the road and up a hill, the home of Great-Uncle Hestus, her grandfather's brother.

Hestus married a tall, skinny, black-haired, spooky woman who always wore black. Great Aunt Clare never came out of her room, except for visitors, or to stand by the road for hours, waiting for the mail at the mailbox. Even in the middle of July, Sam saw Aunt Clare dressed in her best Sunday clothes, topped by a faux-fur coat, waiting by the mailbox in the steamy, red-clay heat of rural Mississippi. Why she did such things, no one ever asked. Clare was tolerated with the same patience one had for a child playing imaginary games.

When Sam's family visited Jasper, they always plodded up Hestus' hill to visit Hestus and Clare. Their house was usually dark, because Clare could not tolerate any light inside. Hestur would lead her to her rocking chair where she never stopped rocking and talking to herself, whispering with her hand over her mouth.

Despite her peculiar behavior, she seemingly had a photographic memory. She recited the age of everyone in the room, what day each was born, the time of the birth, and the location. That was the "conversation" Clare was miraculously able to carry on.

After a while, the men would asked, "How are you feeling today, Miss Clare?" Then they moved on to more pressing issues like cotton and corn, harvesting and planting rituals, and the weather. Rain was a popular topic, either how much it rained recently or how much was expected.

The women were left to the niceties. When Clare was around, Sam's female relatives stared at her nervously. When she recited her facts and figures, they all said, "That's exactly right, Miss Clare."

Eventually, Hestus said, "Miss Clare, you needin' to go back to your room. I believe you is 'tarred' out. We gonna take off yo' dress and git you back in that bed."

Nobody seemed to know why Clare was that way, but there were plenty of rumors. Even after she was placed in the state hospital for the insane down at Whitfield, no one could figure out what was wrong with Clare. Some said she was born that way. Some said Hestus drove her crazy. Some said it happened after she had a baby who died.

Lola said Aunt Clare was stubborn. When a storm came, Lola said, Clare never went into the storm pit, even when everyone else did. At times like that, they placed Aunt Clare in the back of Hestus' old black and rusty Chevrolet and wheeled her down to Whitfield.

She was in and out of the mental hospital for the rest of her life. Hestus told folks it was a shame Aunt Clare could not just stay there, where they had clean, quiet yards. He said it was hard on him.

Hestus died in the car by the side of the road to Ellisville on his way to visit Clare in Whitfield. After someone told Clare the news, she was never allowed to return home or wear her mama's faux-fur coat while waiting for the mail. She stayed in Whitfield until the day she died.

Aunt Clare and Uncle Hestus weren't alone in their struggles. According to rumors in the family, Lola and Papaw Lynn didn't always have the easiest time with each other either. One night, Lola asked him for a shotgun to kill herself. Her younger son Elton shouted, "Jest give it to her this time, Papa. I'm tired of her saying she wants it s'much." Papaw didn't give her a gun, because he was scared what she might do with it.

Mamaw never followed through on her threats, even after she became a widow in 1945 at the age of forty-six. By 1951, she had been living alone without an automobile, running water, electricity, or a phone for six years.

Whenever Sam's father Ben visited Jasper County family, he kept up on their needs and tried to keep them updated on current trends and technological advances. By 1951, Ben saw change coming to Jasper County. Electricity would arrive soon, so he refitted Lola's house in anticipation. Ben bought new white asbestos siding for the exterior of the house and had the inside wired for electricity. Electric lights hung in the middle of the ceiling in each room. He bought Lola an electric cook stove. The old wood stove, used for over thirty years, was carted to the yard. Somebody carried it away.

Mamaw Lola would not have long to enjoy her luxuries. Two weeks after receiving the gift of electricity, she got up one morning around four o'clock to do her ironing with a new electric iron, rather than the fireplace-heated one she had always used. It was her custom to wash, starch, and iron work shirts for her son Elton.

One early morning just after daylight, feeling overly excited, Lola walked toward Elton's house toting his shirts. All alone, she had a stroke. Elton's shirts fell into the dust, as Mamaw hit the ground. She lived another week, in and out of consciousness, at the Methodist hospital in Hattiesburg, the same hospital where Sam and her sister were born.

Lola's embalmed corpse was brought back to her front bedroom the day of the funeral and placed atop one of her handmade quilts. She was the first dead person Sam had ever seen. She wanted to touch Mamaw's. Ben held her up and let her put her hand on Mamaw's face. Sam thought the skin felt like cardboard.

Lola Morgan Cook was buried next to her husband, Ponce de Leon Cook, in the cemetery across the road from Enon Baptist Church. During Lola's funeral, the Baptist minister asked everyone to pass in front of Lola's open casket. From her seat in the front row, Sam watched Lola's sister Patience break down as she approached the body. Screaming and hysterical, Patience had to be assisted back to her pew by her husband and son.

During the funeral, somebody went into Mamaw's house and stole most of her handmade quilts.

Part Two
Hattiesburg

Hattiesburg Roots

Sam often walked alone down the back alley leading to her family's two-story garage apartment on Hardy Street. She sometimes stopped to play in the ditch by the side of the alley with friends who, unlike herself, were mostly tomboys. She preferred, though, to be inside, reading Nancy Drew or The Hardy Boys.

Beginning when Sam was eight years old, her mother allowed her to go alone to the huge downtown library on the bus. She came home with her arms stacked with six or eight mystery novels. She read them all in a week, and returned the next Saturday for another armful. She loved walking up the circular cement steps into the brick library building that had such an original design. It made her feel important and smart.

The building housed her beloved detective mysteries. Her parents did not own books, except the Bible and set of How and Why books for children.

Samantha also loved playing with dolls and paper dolls in her bedroom in the garage apartment. She shared the room with Lilah Jo, who was four-years old. Sam's twin bed sat beside the open window. The best time of year in Hattiesburg was April and May. Sam lay on her bed and thought with the cool, fresh air floating in through the window.

That same year, Sam learned how to cook. Her mother

let her make fudge any time she wanted if they had enough cocoa and sugar. Her dad did not like sweets, so she ate most of it or shared some with Mama, as Sam called Miriam. Soon, Samantha was cooking entire meals, before the age of nine. Ben loved to compliment Sam's cooking while also teasing Miriam by saying that Sam was a better and faster cook than she was. As an adult, Sam wondered if those statements were a cruel jab at his wife.

Close to Sam's apartment and across busy Hardy Street was Oak Lawn Cemetery, the largest and oldest cemetery in the small city. It was not the cemetery where Sam's brother Warren James was buried, which was in one of two newer cemeteries on the city's western edge.

Oak Lawn Cemetery was the final resting place of many of the town's founders. A half block beyond those hundreds of graves, on the other side of the graveyard, lived Sam's friend Alice. Sam's Brownie troop often met at Alice's. Wearing her light-brown uniform and brown felt beanie pinned to her hair with a bobby pin, Samantha walked across the cemetery to reach Alice's. Sometimes after the Scout meeting, the Brownies played on the cemetery grounds.

One afternoon, as Sam headed through the old cemetery after Brownies at Alice's house, she saw something that would forever be emblazoned in her memory as "The Woman in Black." Sam first encountered her among the gray tombstones and green grass in a long, black dress that nearly reached the ground. She wore black gloves, black shoes and a black hat with a black veil. The hat was decorated with a few feathers, and the veil had polka-dots and covered her face.

Frozen in fear, Samantha stared at the woman who strolled through the cemetery, seemingly as comfortably as in her own living room. Sam watched the lady stoop and enter a mausoleum. Eight-year-old Sam was both fearful and curious.

The next week, along with Alice and the other girls in the Brownie troop, Sam set off to find the Lady in Black at the same mausoleum, a word whose meaning Miriam explained.

The troop of girls sneaked across the cemetery, darted in and out among the graves, and peered at the mausoleum from a few feet away, remaining hidden behind tombstones.

They saw the woman inside, sitting beside a stack of magazines. The girls watched, as the woman conversed with a phantom family. They remained silent, as if playing Hide-and-Go-Seek, hearing only their small hearts beating and the sound of their breaths.

"I heard her husband and child are buried there," Alice whispered.

"She's crazy," Brenda said.

"I heard she talks to ghosts," Linda added.

The woman came to the cemetery by bus each morning and stayed all day, or so the girls thought.

One Saturday morning, Sam waited at the bus stop near her home and the cemetery. She planned to go downtown to her beloved, yellow-brick library. The Lady in Black suddenly walked up beside her, as if appearing from thin air, and Sam started shaking. She almost ran home to the garage apartment to Mama. But the pull of the library was too strong.

Sam needed to get to the library to check out another of the orange-colored biography such as Susan B. Anthony, another mystery of Nancy Drew or the Hardy Boys. She especially liked the biographies such as Florence Nightingale or Joan of Arc. She had read many such books already and loved them — the tales of heroic women. She read many such books as a little white girl in Hattiesburg, although black children were not allowed into this building. It never occurred to Samantha to wonder whether they had a library of their own.

Back at the bus stop, the tall skinny lady looked down at Sam and said, "You are a pretty little girl. I had a little girl like you. But she died. Her father died too. I come here every day and read to them. Sam did not smile or speak. "I am not your little girl," she thought. "Stay away from me. I am not dead."

When the bus came, Sam was so very glad she could step up to its steps and go a completely different direction from the lady in Black. She watched through the window, as the bus pulled away, taking her away from the eerie woman who waited for another bus to take her home, where no one waited for her.

Early 1940s

The sound of a train whistle filled their ears in 1944. Sam was two years old.

"Sam!" Miriam called. Sam later wondered if the incessant sound of a train so close to their duplex made Miriam miss her home and family in California.

Sam looked up and smiled at her mother. "Mama," she said happily.

"Sam, here comes the train. Let's go wave to the soldiers." She took her daughter's sandy hand—Sam had been playing in her "sandbox"—in her warm one, and they waved at the soldiers who rode down the track that was parallel to the side street that rad beside their duplex.

"Where are they're going, Mama?" Sam asked. "On their maneuvers," Miriam answered.

Sam had no idea what that strange word meant. But she liked the men, who wore ice-cream hats and crisp khaki uniforms and who waved from the diesel train. Sometimes she saw them on the main street of Hattiesburg. What Miriam did not mention was that the men were headed to the east coast to ship out for points overseas. Some would never return. There was a lot Sam did not understand in those days.

In her later years, Samantha Ann Cook would still be filled with, and fascinated by, her earliest childhood memories that shaped her into the woman she became. Samantha's skin was almost translucent with age, and her years were worn from marriage, teaching, writing, parenting, and grand-parenting.

The smallest life events transported Sam's mind to stories from her childhood. One particular day, Sam flipped through a batch of current Easter photos she picked up from Walgreens. She smiled at an image of her only granddaughter, aged two-and-a half. The child was wearing a ruffled pink Easter dress. Her mouth was stuffed with Easter candy. Her brown, wide-set, fawn-like eyes twinkled over a beautifully shaped, full-lipped, rose-colored mouth.

The picture reminded Samantha of a time when she wore a dress about the same size. As a little tot, she was the darling little flower girl in two consecutive summer weddings, the first when she was twenty-months old, and the next when she was three. Both weddings took place in the southern California San Joaquin desert. Sam and her mother, Miriam, traveled there together, departing from their home in Mississippi, then riding from New Orleans to Los Angeles on the Sunset Limited to reach California where most of Miriam's family lived. The dress for the first wedding was handmade, white-crocheted, and embroidered with pink roses and green leaves. It was tailored especially for her in California, with her mother sending measurements from Mississippi. The dress was accessorized with a light-blue, crocheted, wide-brimmed hat, trimmed in matching pink flowers and edged with wire to preserve the round shape, tied under little Samantha's chin with a blue ribbon.

The second dress was pink taffeta with a long, gathered, net skirt patterned with large silver circles. Sam wore each of these dresses only once, prancing down the aisles, strewing rose petals and feeling proud.

Miriam kept both outfits preserved in plastic bags until long after Sam was an adult and married. They were eventually given away. Sam did not remember why she and her mother decided to part with them. She wished very much they hadn't. She hoped someone loved and used them.

Those train trips to the California desert began when Sam was less than a year old. Miriam's family had migrated to California in the late 1920s, looking for work. With a few exceptions, they all returned to Mississippi in 1933. Later, though, they trekked West again, except for Miriam, who by that time, had married Ben Cook. During Sam's childhood, Miriam pined for her family in California and traveled there to see them as often as possible, which was usually once every two years.

When Sam was a baby, she and her mother went alone on one of those long train rides. Miriam did not bear the brunt of holding her infant alone, though. It was 1943. With World War II in progress, there were plenty of soldiers on the train who loved the smiling baby. They passed her around to give Miriam a break while she made bottles or washed up in the bathroom.

Since she did not have the money to afford a private bedroom on the train, Miriam held her infant all through the night during the 2,000-mile journey until they reached Los Angeles, where Miriam's sister, Virginia, and her husband, Denzil, met them, with their two daughters. They all squeezed into Virginia and Denzil's car and drove over "The Ridge," the chain of mountains just before entering the San Joaquin Valley. Several other family members lived near Virginia in the desert, oil-rich town of Taft, which is near Bakersfield. In later years, whenever Sam's family drove out to visit, Ben Cook always said as he started home, "I didn't lose anything in Taft, California, that's for sure."

By the time Samantha was old enough to remember those trips, her little sister, Lilah Jo, came along, too. By then, Miriam could afford a bedroom on the Sunset Limited, where they could sleep and wash themselves.

Sleeping on the train in their clothing on bunk beds that turned into a couch during the day, with their own private lavatory and toilet, Samantha had her first feeling of elegance. Their meals were taken in the dining car, where Sam first encountered bran muffins while eating on linen table-cloths and being served by Black porters.

Sam loved those train rides across the western desert. Back then, children did not have electronic toys to keep them entertained. Although she loved to read, she was not allowed to bring books. She stared out the window to pass the time. When they went through West Texas, the large white letters E-L P-A-S-0 carved into the mountain fascinated her. How did they get there? The train blew its whistle all through the arid Arizona heat. The sand, mirages, and Joshua cacti entranced Samantha.

Miriam and Sam were glad the Sunset Limited had become air-conditioned. Sam never tired of the desert scenery, and those biannual, two-day and two-night trips with her mother and Lilah. Wondering and watching prompted Samantha to love the desert for the rest of her life.

Sam was born in Hattiesburg, Mississippi, on November 28, 1942. She came into the world with thick, straight, black hair. It fell out within a few months and was replaced by blonde curls. As a newborn, her skin was so dark, that she had a line of pigmentation between her palm and her outside skin. Miriam thought her daughter looked like a Black child, except for the straight hair. Sam's eyes eventually turned bright blue-green, which complemented her blonde hair.

Samantha was born thirteen months after her brother, James Warren Cook, had died. Samantha's birth date and James's death date were the same. Ben and Miriam had named their ill-fated child after Miriam's only brother, James. The middle name, Warren, was for the middle name of Miriam's father.

James Warren was a "blue baby," a term for a baby born with a congenital heart defect. To repair the defect, he needed open-heart surgery, which was not performed in 1941. The most-telling symptom of a blue baby was a blue complexion caused by lack of oxygen. The first successful blue-baby operation was completed in 1944, three years after Miriam's first child died in the hospital after living three hours.

Benjamin Warren Cook was a short man with a big personality. At five-foot-eight, he seemed to shrink as he grew older, his black hair thinning with age. Toward the end of his life he had more bald head than hair, revealing his skull and his age spots against his olive-colored skin. He was never in good physical shape, which made sense, because his past times were fishing and hunting, neither of which provided much of a workout.

Ben was an extrovert, usually smiling through his thick lips. He joined and led several civic clubs during his adult life, and often became the president of the group. When people spoke of him they would say, "Ben Cook never met a stranger!" But that was his public life.

At home, he was sometimes irritable and had a temper. Like most people, he had secret childhood baggage he grappled with and as an adult he hid his sorry for the rest of the world. Ben buried his first child accompanied only by two male friends and the minister. No family came to the funeral. The gravestone had an inscription that read Cook: Infant Son Oct. 21, 1941. Ben cried every day for weeks.

Miriam was unable to see her son buried. She stayed in bed for the sanctioned two weeks of hospital stay after childbirth, listening to the sounds of new motherhood coming from the other side of the room that she shared with another woman. The other woman's baby was born alive and was doing well. Her depression was compounded by the long stay in hospital and perhaps from lack of compassion from the male doctors. Miriam suspected that they never considered how she must feel, lying in bed alone, while another mother nursed and cuddled her child.

After he stopped weeping, Ben never discussed James. Miriam always spoke of her to Sam and Lilah as "her first baby."

World War II was underway in other parts of the World when the U .S. entered the war in December,1941, following the bombing of Pearl Harbor. Ben had a physical deferment and was not required to serve in the armed forces.

When Sam was born a little over a year after James died, Samantha was born. Had she been a boy, her name would have been the same as her dead brother's, a decision her parents had made.

When Sam was born, Hattiesburg had a population of about 30,000, but it felt bigger due to the nearby military post, Camp Shelby, a training site for soldiers. The camp is still there, with its large, artificial lake sprawled slightly west of Highway 49, towards Gulfport.

Hattiesburg was a typical small Southern city, sectioned off by class and color lines. The Cook family home was a meager four room duplex straddling the line between poverty and riches. Their apartment faced the graveled block of Fourth Avenue, just off the opulent Pine Street, which ran through Hattiesburg and was part of the North-South Highway 11. That was the street where Samantha eventually played with her best childhood friend while simultaneously feeling the sting of her own family's lack of possessions.

On the other side of the train tracks adjacent to Sam's apartment building lived some of the city's poorer white residents. The children from that neighborhood attended a less-affluent elementary school than the one Samantha eventually attended. Camp Elementary School was said to be the best elementary school in Hattiesburg before Woodley Elementary was built near the University of Southern Mississippi. Camp School took up an entire block in the middle of the older part of Hattiesburg.

In some of Sam's earliest memories, she was three-years old, playing in a sandbox in the yard, while her mother watched from the kitchen window. They often heard the faint rumble of a train. Sam filled the pail with shovels of sand, which cascaded halfway into the bucket with the rest covering her chubby legs. Sam, ignoring the sand, worked busily at her task.

Miriam had a favorite outfit for Sam. She often dressed her in light-blue corduroy overalls, which kept the sand out of Sam's panties. Her white bonnet, to keep away too much sun, tied under her chin, fell away from her face.

Sam remembered her mother leaning over, adjusting her hat so that her face would not get sun-burned. Sam's olive complexion was like her father's, but unlike him, her skin darkened easily in the sun, probably due to some Choctaw heritage on Miriam's side of the family. There were family rumors that some relatives intermarried with Native Americans. Though those were only whispers, Miriam's high cheekbones, which she inherited from her father, suggested the rumors might be true.

Miriam was a slim, stylish woman, who wore her dark, wavy hair long in a chignon, pulled back from her face at the sides with combs. She had large high bangs. At five-feet-six-inches tall, she was only two inches shorter than her husband. She did not want to be taller than he, so she rarely wore high heels.

Sam did not know it then, but the Black men, or "help," built Sam's wooden sandbox. Her father never built anything or did any maintenance. He was more interested in numbers and money. He worked as a bookkeeper at a local car dealership. He made sure they had what they needed. He lovingly oversaw the construction of the sandbox, where Sam could play alone and be watched out the kitchen window by Miriam.

Hattiesburg's Religions

Despite the war and a mother who still mourned the loss of her first child, Sam had a happy time during her first four-and-a half years. Before her little sister was born, she had her mother all to herself. They spent days singing, reading, memorizing nursery rhymes, playing outside, and walking into town for groceries.

Many of Miriam's days were spent readying Sam's bedroom for their next tenant. The renters they welcomed were some of the many wives or girlfriends of the soldiers stationed at Camp Shelby. The women came from around the U.S. to be near their men before they were shipped off to war.

Renting Samantha's room netted the family five dollars a week, which enhanced the family's income and provided a home for the women who shared a kitchen and small bathroom. Many women who stayed with the Cooks worked as much-needed nurses at the local Methodist hospital, where all three Cook children were born.

Sam's mother remembered one particular renter, a Jewish woman from New York, named Rivkah. She traveled to Hattiesburg to see her fiance while he was stationed at Camp Shelby. Having corresponded with her through letters, Miriam and Ben knew that Rivkah was Jewish. Most Christians, Protestant or Catholic, would not rent to or socialize with

Jews, but the Cooks needed the money.

In the days before Rivkah's arrival, Sam listened, as her mother talked about what would be like living with a Jew. She believed Jews were all damned to hell for rejecting Jesus and she mostly felt sorry for them.

Amazingly, however, Rivkah became Miriam's favorite renter, though that did not change her beliefs about the eternal damnation of Jews. Miriam probably tried not to think about it while the jovial and energetic young woman played with Samantha. Rivkah did not have a paid job, as many of the renters did, so she had lots of free time to spend with Sam.

A playful, dark-haired young woman who smiled often, Rivkah added a delightful energy to the Cooks' home. Wildly fond of Samantha, she spent hours reading to and playing with Sam.

She taught her the verses to all the classic children's songs and rhymes, including Mary Had a Little Lamb; Row, Row, Row Your Boat; Little Bo Peep; and many others. When Miriam and Ben had company, they wanted Samantha to show off her reciting skills. The precocious child performed for friends and family at social gatherings whenever given the chance.

Samantha was an extrovert like her father. She "never met a stranger," as people said about Ben Cook. This aspect of her personality made her entertainment even more lively. Miriam also delighted in dressing up her adorable, blonde daughter like a doll. One of Sam's favorite outfits was a wine-colored velvet dress with a white lace collar, which was paired with high-top shoes and white socks. When dressed in that suit, Sam knew it was time to recite and show off. She showcased her verses by reciting every nursery rhyme she knew, which were many. Afterwards, Sam received adoration and praise from the adults who watched.

Though Rivkah became a positive presence in the household, renting to her also came with risk. Hattiesburg was no different than many small Southern towns whose citizens held prejudicial views in the 1940s. While Sam and her mother were having fun with their Jewish renter, many Jews who came to Camp Shelby with army partners were not able to find places to rent in town.

When Sam was an adult, some of her Jewish friends said that they slept in their cars for many days in Hattiesburg until they found an open-minded landlord. The prejudice toward Jews surrounding Samantha during and after World War II was something she thought little about as a child. As an adult, she wondered how the White townspeople justified it.

Prejudice never truly makes sense. Much of Hatties-burg's economy depended upon Jewish business owners. The town boasted several department stores with Jewish owners. Fine's, Eiseman's, and Belk's not only provided needed goods, mainly women's clothes and shoes, but also offered many coveted jobs.

Some of the medical doctors were Jewish, too. After the war, many Jews migrated to the South, and there was an in-creasingly large Jewish population per capita in Hattiesburg, large enough to support an active synagogue.

While Miriam had a personal relationship with Rivkah, she found it difficult to reconcile her feelings with her beliefs about salvation. Miriam always found it odd, even to herself, that she was so enraptured with her Jewish tenant. She also greatly admired Dr. Eisenstein, an optometrist her family adored, especially after he solved a problem Sam had with recurring eye infections.

Miriam had a powerful belief system. She began ear-ly life as a Pentecostal Christian and remained so for many years, especially during Sam's youth. The Assembly of God Church that Miriam attended in Hattiesburg was filled with poor Pentecostals, clashing with the distinctly more mid-dle-class Fifth Avenue Baptist Church parishioners, where Ben worshipped. When it came to religion, the Cooks were a divided family. Ben and Miriam took turns taking Samantha to their respective churches.

Sam remembered one Sunday morning in particular when she and her mother crunched across the gravel road on their way to the First Assembly of God. It was Miriam's turn to take Samantha to church. Located on Bernice Avenue, the First Assembly of God was on the southern edge of town, far from their duplex near Fourth Avenue. Sometimes, Ben dropped them off, but that day, he was running late to his own church service and dropped them at the Methodist Hospital. They had to walk the final mile.

The area of town near the church would eventually become a slum. The weather that day was nice enough, and Miriam, who was pregnant, told Sam that she enjoyed the stroll. In a few months, it would be harder to take long walks with two children instead of one.

They usually drove past the Catholic Church on the way to their church, and Miriam always pointed to it and told Samantha, "It's so sad the lies they teach those little children about statues being holy. There's only one Holy One, and that's Jesus, but there's no way for those kids to know that."

Miriam never passed up an opportunity to educate her daughter, and later, her baby sister, on the evils of Catholicism. Being a fundamentalist, Pentecostal Christian, she believed only one group of religious folk were scarier than Jews: Catholics.

Later in life, Miriam warned Sam of the dangers of marrying into such a religion. "Samantha, I'd rather you married a Jew than a Catholic. At least Jews have a second chance at being saved, according to Scripture." Samantha married neither a Jew nor a Catholic.

Sam listened closely, as her mother talked against Catholics. She came to think that some spooky hocus-pocus was going on in that church. For years, she wondered about the bizarre ceremonies the Catholics had in the sanctum. She could never find the right words to ask her mother why she believed as she did about Catholics. She always had a yen to visit the church to see, but she never did.

Miriam and Sam arrived at the white wooden building that housed the First Assembly of God. They entered what was termed the "auditorium," which was never called a "sanctuary," and which had descending seating from back to front. They walked down the aisles on the hard rubber mat covering the hardwood floors between wooden pews.

Sitting, Sam stared down at the altar and pulpit at the lowest level of the sloping room. The pulpit sat before the choir and loft, where a picture of Jesus looked down divinely upon the congregation. Across the room, folding doors closed off the adult Sunday school rooms. Above, the tongue-in-groove hardwood paneled ceiling gave the house of worship a mystical feel.

Sam sat beside her mother, swinging her chubby, four-year old legs. "Sam," Miriam murmured, placing a hand on her daughter. Sam stopped swinging and looked at her. Then she leaned in for a hug and softly slid her tiny across her mother's pregnant belly. Another child was coming soon.

"It's time to pray," her mother whispered. They bowed their heads. The church began an incantation as a group, with everyone praying out loud.

"Father God, oh Jesus, oh Jesus, please forgive us our sins." The repetitive droning bored Sam. She clung to her mother's side, leaned against her, and looked around at the bowed heads. A female congregant broke through the incantation, speaking in tongues. It seemed to Sam that the same woman did that every Sunday. Her eyes closed, her mouth opened, and something that sounded like words, but were unintelligible, spewed forth as if she could not control herself. Everyone else grew silent.

Sam felt a little scared. She was never sure what it all meant. Apparently, neither did anyone else. When the woman was relieved of the supernatural elocution, another woman, who must have been an expert in spiritual syntax, stood and said, "Thus saith the Lord." She went on to interpret the speech for the rest of the congregation. The message was too cryptic for a four-year-old to understand.

When they finished praying, they sang. Sam enjoyed that part of church. The next part, though, she found ridiculous. As a group, they paraded around the church. Sam remembered one hymn entitled Hold the Fort. The hymn ended with the words, Wave the banner back to Heaven, by Thy grace we will.

She joined the parade, though she felt silly. As was customary, she reached into her pocket and pulled out her handkerchief, as they neared the chorus. She waved it in the air, parading around the church auditorium as if she were entering Heaven and needed to wave her flag, or banner as the song implied, to signal to God that she was coming. She felt self-conscious doing that, but she did it. It was expected.

Miriam sat, holding Lilah Jo, watching Samantha wave her banner, and smiled at her daughter's performance, not knowing that Sam felt it was quite foolish. Miriam never felt comfortable participating in theatrics. She never spoke in tongues. Later, she told Sam she never felt the urge to seek that spiritual gift. The spirit never entered her that way.

For Miriam, clinging to Pentecostalism was not necessarily a matter of faith but more a family tradition. The irony of being married to a Baptist, who opposed the Pentecostal approach, was that Miriam's own father was once a Baptist preacher who diverged from his faith, taking his large family down a new spiritual path.

Miriam's father, Rowan Divan Stringer, converted from Southern Baptist to pentecostalism when he moved the family from Mississippi to California. In the San Joaquin Desert, Rowan began speaking in tongues. During his early days as a Baptist preacher, he invited disciples of Aimee McPherson to hold a "West Coast Tent Revival" at his church. McPherson was a Los Angeles-based female evangelist in the 1920s and 1930s. She founded the Foursquare Church, a protestant, evangelical, pentecostal Christian church. That denomination was quite different from what Rowan Stringer was accustomed to.

One Sunday afternoon, after his own church services ended, two Foursquare Church preachers, a man and a woman, entered his church complete with their own audience. They spoke about the power and gift of the Spirit, based on

Acts 2:4: "And they were all filled with the Holy Ghost and began to speak with other tongues, as the Spirit gave them utterance."

When the female preacher spoke, she closed her eyes and vocalized in a manner Rowan had never before witnessed. A fire stirred within him, and he wanted to know more.

Next, a male preacher spoke about the "full Gospel," as he described I Corinthians 12:10. "To another the working of miracles; to another prophecy; to another the discerning of spirits; to another diverse kinds of tongues; to another the interpretation of tongues."

Rowan witnessed the preacher speaking in tongues. He closed his eyes, and his face morphed into a sweet, painful expression, as words that made no sense to Rowan's native English flowed from his mouth. It was clear that it was something the two preachers could not control. As they ended their sessions, they became emotional, as if something of their human form had been released.

For Rowan, a flame was lit. The day wore on, but he could not stop thinking about what he had witnessed. He wanted it for himself. When he went home that evening, his family was scattered about. His six children played and shouted. His wife cooked with a fussy baby on her hip. A pleading expression came to her face when her husband entered the house after being away all day.

All he wanted was quiet, so he swiftly went out to seclude himself in his study shed in the backyard, as he did often when moved by his own thoughts. He sat in his chair and began reading the Bible in the original Greek, a language he had mastered. He began praying. As he did, suddenly, a word came to him and moved through his mouth, as if it were not his own. He felt his mouth open. Words poured out, words he never heard before and whose meaning was unknown. It lasted for only a short time; but, when it ended, Rowan felt something powerful flowing within his mind and body.

He knew he would quit his life as a Baptist preacher and become a pentecostal at any cost. He had been baptized in the Holy Spirit. As his family would come to learn, this change came at a great cost to all of them.

Shortly afterwards, Rowan Stringer was born again as a pentecostal Christian in the Assembly of God denomination. Pentecostals took the experiences of the disciples in the "upper room" after Christ ascended to be available to all. This included speaking in tongues and divine healing. Other people sometimes derisively referred to them as Holy Rollers.

While Rowan's spiritual life may have changed, his personal transformation had an unfavorable effect on the rest of his family. Pentecostals were poor during the Depression, so Rowan never made a decent salary from pastoring.

He often left his wife and six children for weeks at a time, supposedly attending revivals. That was what he told his wife, who was eighteen years younger. She wondered if his extended trips away from family were truly for religion. Rowan never seemed built for family life. Even before he married, he once abandoned his original family for ten years, from the time when he was twenty to the age of thirty.

Leta Boyd Stringer found ways to feed her children when her husband was gone, though their finances were always scant. She made do without Rowan by taking in ironing and selling her hens' eggs.

When the children were starving, her mother sent Miriam and her siblings out in the dusty streets of the desert town of Taft, California, to watch for the food wagon. That was a Depression-era fixture offering goods rejected by local grocery stores. Filled with second-rate food from stores, this was handed out to people up and down the streets. Leta and her children cherished those rejected goods. Often they had little or nothing else to eat.

When there were not enough vegetables from the food wagon or their garden, Leta and her children ate home-baked bread and "clabber," a yogurt-like substance, which was basically curdled milk for supper. To make it edible, they added a little sugar, nutmeg, and cinnamon. The food wagon vegetables were eaten for lunch, while clabber was dinner.

If they were lucky, they had chicken during the weekend, slaughtered by Leta from her henhouse, and vegetables from their garden.

Such a life of poverty was not what her Boyd parents had imagined for their second daughter. Rowan's defection of his faith and the desertion of his family for long stretches were an embarrassment. It shamed them. Leta's parents were Sally Ann Gulledge and Ephraim Boyd. They were particularly displeased by Rowan's treatment of Leta and her six children. They settled in nearby San Jose to be near another daughter until Ephraim died of a heart attack. He was taken home to Mississippi for burial on a weeklong train ride. Sally Ann went along and stayed with her oldest daughter, Tera, for a year in McComb, Mississippi. Tera was the only one of Leta's siblings who had not migrated to California.

The Boyds were staunch Baptists. Ephraim was the music director in the Bogue Chitto Baptist Church. Having a pentecostal son-in-law was an embarrassment to their social standing and religious beliefs. They never cared for Rowan, anyway. His actions, which they despised, only bolstered their original perception of him. The Stringers, Rowan's family, eventually became outcasts to the Boyds and remain that way until the present day. Four generations later, many of Samantha's cousins are still pentecostal and believe in the Holy Ghost and the gifts of the Spirit, all because of Rowan Stringer's conversion. His daughter, Miriam, for a long time clung to pentecostalism despite her father's choosing beliefs over family. But Miriam's husband, Ben, persisted in his own Baptist beliefs.

Miriam and Ben's respective stubbornness had them fighting over Sam's path to salvation. Which church would their little daughter attend? With both parents digging in their heels, they finally reached a compromise in a non-legally binding, religious custodial agreement. Sam would be traded off every other week.

One week she would go with her mother on Sunday mornings, while her daddy took her to his church on Sunday nights. The next week, she went with her father in the morning and her mother at night.

After Lilah Jo was born, maternal power won out. Ben tried to take both girls for a while, but he found he could not manage dueling children during church services, especially with one in diapers. Sam's little sister was a fussy child. She did not want anyone but her parents to touch or hold her.

Even after Lilah Jo put a wrench into their regular routine, Ben still took his daughters to church occasionally. The final straw came when Samantha was baptized. Miriam insisted Sam be baptized in the Assembly of God Church. In many protestant denominations, children are not baptized at birth but only when they make an individual decision to "follow Jesus" and declare their intentions. One day at church with Miriam, Sam "walked down the aisle" in response to the invitation and made it known she wanted to follow Jesus. The next step was baptism.

Since their church building had no baptisimal, the baptism ceremony was conducted at a stagnant pond on a Sunday afternoon at 4:00 p.m. when Sam was eight-years old. Ben refused to attend the baptism, but he finally realized just how insistent his wife was about her beliefs. He gave up and relinquished both little girls to accompany their mother to church. They did not worship as a family together until later, when they moved to another town.

Sam's mother's fundamentalism held firm, however, even in the Baptist Church. When they were adults, Lilah Jo told Sam that when Lilah was seven, she ran into the middle of the street one dark night, because their mother scolded her that "God sees everything you do." She wanted to hide from His eyes. Perhaps if she ran from the house into the blackness, He couldn't see her so well.

The religion of the California relatives was so implanted in their nature that on their visits, Lilah Jo thought God lived in the trees there, or perhaps in the clouds. She always thought they crossed into another country when they crossed the state line. The family members discussed God in the most terrifying way, and Lilah was filled with fear. Sam did not like the God talk among that church group but was glad to have a mother, and a church, and she was not frightened. She did not believe everything the others said, anyway. Then and always, she went her own way.

The Mansion on Pine Street

Samantha's other best friend, Cissie Goodrich, lived only two houses down. Although she was in such close proximity, she was in an entirely different type of neighborhood. Playtime with Cissie was worlds away from Sam's days spent hidden in the backyard of her tiny duplex with Miranda.

The gravelly Fourth Avenue, where the Cook family lived, was barely on the better side of the railroad track that separated them from a poorer neighborhood. A dark stucco house owned by Mrs. Lipscomb, the grandmother of a devilish boy named Ricky, stood alone between the Cooks' four-room duplex and the Goodrichs' grand mansion. The Lipscomb house and the duplex that the Cooks shared with the Graces were the only two homes on their side of a very short block of Fourth Avenue that was just off old, affluent Pine Street, part of US Highway 11.

Pine Street boasted towering mansions and canopied trees, with all the signs of prosperous growth over many generations. The plush thoroughfare was also the main boulevard through Hattiesburg. There, Cissie Goodrich and her family resided as a multigenerational group in the home of Cissie's grandmother, Aylen Le Blanc. Aylen's husband, a builder who came to Hattiesburg from New Orleans, constructed the one-floor, eight-thousand-square-foot mansion, as he did many of the finer structures in Hattiesburg. Cissie later told Sam that her grandfather built the house to sell as a spec house, but, when her grandmother saw how it looked when it was finished, she wanted to enjoy the space and graciousness herself.

Aylen was the matriarch of the clan. Her husband, Cissie's grandfather and builder of the great home, had passed away. Also living there were Audri and Charles, Cissie's parents, and Bubba and Peden, Cissie's brothers. The Le Blancs had three daughters, with one lived on the Mississippi Coast and seldom visited.

The children called their parents Audri and Charles and never said "Momma" or "Daddy" as most Southern children did. They called their grandmother, Aylen, by her first name, too.

Together, the mother-daughter duo of Aylen and Audri kept up the great house. Sam never witnessed any hired help in their home, though they surely could have afforded it. She wondered why they never had a Black servant woman, which most upper-class Mississippians considered necessary in those days.

Aylen raised flowers from bulbs and seeds from around the world, including orange poppies, purple thrift, begonias, pansies, hibiscus, and daisies, filling the yard with just about any color one could imagine. Each day, mother and daughter cooked a large noon meal before retiring to the sun porch on the side of the house in the afternoons. Audri, recovering from her morning work, sometimes did needlework with the windows open and the attic fan spinning.

Sometimes, they had visitors over to play bridge.

While Aylen and Audri kept the house, Cissie's father, Charles Goodrich, worked in a tire shop. Sam hardly ever saw him, but her own father, Ben, was a well-suited friend to Charles. They lived near each other, their businesses were next door to each other, and they enjoyed hunting and fishing together.

Sam adored playing at Cissie's house, which had four

huge bedrooms and two bathrooms. Darkly stained oak panel woodwork lined the walls in the entire house, including the kitchen, dining room, and the long hallway that led to the living room, which was always closed, except during Aylen's formal bridge parties. The grand house's dark paneling made it feel cool and quiet. It was both spooky and wonderful.

Cissie's parents had the bedroom in the middle of the house, which opened three ways — to the hall by the guest bathroom, to the boys' bedroom, and to the private sunroom that Aylen frequently used.

Sam's favorite spot was the attic playroom, which had been built for Audri when she was a child. That was where Cissie housed her dolls and where the girls could be secluded from Cissie's mean brothers, who had their own playroom downstairs. Bubba, the elder brother, was calm, but the younger one was nicknamed "Rascal" by his mother. He eventually grew up to be a pediatrician in Jackson, Mississippi, though he retained the nickname.

Cissie had a second playroom in the backyard, a real playhouse that had also been her mother's. When Sam and Cissie weren't playing in one of the many playrooms, they entertained themselves in Cissie's bedroom, a spacious room in the front of the house with yellow wallpaper, twenty-foot ceilings, and antique furniture. Sam often thought her own apartment would easily fit inside Cissie's bedroom with room to spare. Feeling the sting of her family's lack of possessions, she never wanted to return home to their meager abode.

Sam typically entered Cissie's grand world through the back porch, which was like a small office where they kept the telephone. The area outside the home was perfect for children's play, too. Cissie and Sam loved sitting on the front porch beside the majestic porte cochere where Aylen usually parked her car, which she never learned to drive. It gave the house the feel of a grand hotel. The two girls situated themselves on the wooden porch swing, counting passing cars, swinging, and singing silly songs to pass the time during long summer days. Sometimes, they played in the cool of the porte cochere if Aylen's car wasn't there.

When Aylen was home, Sam relished watching her work in the majestic flowerbeds filled with exotic blooms, always wearing a big straw sunhat. Aylen's gardens extended inside the silver-gated fence, along the back of the house, and all along the sunny western side, where she grew her California poppies. Samantha thought they were the most wonderful flowers she had ever seen, with their long-stemmed bright oranges, yellows, and reds.

One afternoon, as the girls swung on the porch, they peeked inside the window to see Audri setting up for a bridge game in the living room. The room, filled with large, formal antiques from New Orleans, was strictly off limits to children, but the parties looked like so much fun. Several card tables were set up, and Aylen served tea, cookies, and petite sandwiches to her guests in the dining room before the games commenced. Sam dreamed of being invited to those fancy parties, but unfortunately, like the living room, they were for adults only.

At Last, Beloved School

In 1940s Hattiesburg, first grade was the first year of public school, while kindergarten was offered as a private school option. Cissie and several of her friends went to a half-day kindergarten down the block on Pine Street in an old mansion. During the day while Cissie was away, Samantha was bored. She waited outside on the steps of the duplex for Cissie to return.

Sam's parents couldn't afford kindergarten, just as they weren't able to afford tap or ballet lessons, which she couldn't have taken, anyway, since Miriam thought any form of dancing was a sin. Many of Sam's days were spent playing alone in the backyard.

Sometimes, Lilah Jo joined her, sitting in her stroller or in Mrs. Grace's double stroller with Oogie. Sam sometimes pushed them to the corner by Cissie's house and back. Her mother and Mrs. Grace trusted her with the babies. If one of them cried, she always brought them home.

With nothing better to do, Sam sometimes stared at her little sister, a thin, delicate child. Lilah Jo had the most beautiful corn-silk, white-blonde hair anyone had ever seen. Her ears stuck out, and she drooled. Sam knew better than to try to pick her up. Lilah Jo would scream, and then her mother would become angry with Sam for upsetting the baby.

But the first day of first grade quickly approached. It was 1948. Sam was five and a half, and she could not wait to go to school! She could mostly read already, because her mother had taught her. To prepare for first grade, Miriam bought Sam new school clothes, a Brownie uniform, paper, pencils, and scissors.

Samantha would enter Camp Elementary School, the best school in Hattiesburg at the time. Sam felt lucky to attend Camp. If her family had lived just one block down and across the tracks, she would have gone to a less affluent school instead. Sam lived just inside the boundary, so she went to school with Cissie, along with the wealthiest children from the most prestigious families in the entire city of Hattiesburg.

The neighborhood surrounding Camp was sheer paradise. There were classic Southern homes and gorgeous old oak trees everywhere. The cinder-block school was painted a soothing cream and its campus occupied an entire block.

Outside, the campus lawn was covered not with grass but with red dirt, and the areas was dotted with playground equipment, including swings and monkey bars. One side of Camp was bordered by woods, and Sam and her friends quickly learned to play along the edge of the woods during their long recesses.

Sam used her hands to sweep up pine straw to make playhouses. The pine straw made the walls, and Sam dug up green moss to create a yard. They also loved to play hopscotch and jump rope on the sidewalk in front of the school.

Camp School had hardwood floors, and, under the windows, steam heaters provided warmth during the winter. There was no air-conditioning, so the windows were always open during hot weather. The first through third grades were on the first floor, while the fourth and fifth grades were on the second. When Sam started school, it occurred to her that children in the other classes weren't as smart as those in her class, and she later learned that each grade was split into two classes based on test scores and IQ. Sam always placed in the class with the brighter students.

Samantha finally felt like part of the school crowd. Every day, she and Cissie walked the five blissful blocks to school together. As an adult, Sam thought back on those days as some of the most beautiful of her life, even the rainy days when they wore red or yellow galoshes. Sometimes, neighborhood girls who were part of their crowd joined them, like Faye, Alice, or Patsy. Sometimes Cissie's friend Irene would join them, too. She was in their Brownie troop, but Sam never knew her very well.

At that age, their crowd didn't exclude anyone based on economic class. Faye, who often had no buttons on her clothes, seemed poor. Alice, with her long, dishwater-brown hair, was unkempt. Patsy, with her medium-length, curly, black hair, moved easily with any set, but her mother always seemed so sad. Sam eventually learned that Patsy's father been "killed in action," though she wasn't sure what that meant.

The two girls in the group who Sam thought were definitely rich were Cissie and Sandra Toussaint. Sandra, Sam reasoned, had to be rich, maybe even richer than Cissie, because she always wore brand-new dresses. Her father was one of the main lawyers in Hattiesburg. Her mother didn't venture out of doors much and never visited Camp School. Some people said she drank most of the day.

Samantha's friends were mostly female, as were her teachers. It was during this time in history that women began taking over the ranks of school teaching in the United States, replacing the men during wartime.

By 1948, when Sam began first grade, the war had been over for three years, and veterans had returned in droves, looking for work. The women who filled their places in schools, factories, or ammunition depots, or who worked for the WAVs or in officers' clubs, were encouraged to give up their jobs to return home and be housewives, whether or not they had children.

Sam's first-grade teacher, Miss Myrick, went to the local teachers college, as had many of the teachers at Camp School. The teachers colleges in the Deep South were typically small, non-coed schools that taught the teaching profession to women only. Once they married, there was some concern they might face unemployment if a younger female teacher or a male teacher from before the war needed a job. Thus, they were admonished never to marry, or if they did, to keep it a secret.

None of Sam's teachers were married except Miss Myrick, a rebel who married at Christmas. She didn't tell anyone, but somehow everyone found out through whispers and rumors.

"Did you know Miss Myrick got married?" the students asked.

The children never knew her married name. She was always "Miss Myrick" to Sam and her classmates.

Rebel though she was, Miss Myrick was thorough and strict. If the children, particularly the boys, talked in class, she wrote their names on the blackboard to let them know they had to stay after school.

Detention slips were handed out most often during the daily rest period, when all students were required to lay their heads on their desks and stay totally quiet. Miss Myrick was the one who most needed rest. There was rarely an entirely quiet rest period. The boys in particular managed to get themselves in trouble, but Sam wasn't immune to trouble, either.

One afternoon, Samantha floated around the room, whispering, "Shhh, Miss Myrick needs to rest." Shortly afterward, Sam saw Miss Myrick write her name on the blackboard. Miss Myrick didn't realize Sam was being Miss Goody-Goody, and Samantha's feelings were hurt tremendously.

"How unfair!" she cried to her mother when she got home that afternoon. "I was only trying to help!"

Along with such disciplinary tactics, Sam also remembered Miss Myrick for being one of the mentors in her life who encouraged her creativity. Sam received a dose of encouragement from her that lasted her entire life.

One day, Miss Myrick handed out strips of newspaper

and bowls of flour and water, then returned to her desk at the front of the classroom, heels clicking in a brisk walk. Her skirt flounced as she took a seat. She picked up a bowl and demonstrated how to mix the water and flour into glue. Then, she showed the class how to paint it carefully onto the strips of paper. Miss Myrick expected each student to create their own papier-mâché animal.

As Sam watched her teacher demonstrate the craft, she sat paralyzed at her desk frantically trying to think of an animal. Actions were better than staring, so Sam formed what she thought looked like an animal. After some time, Miss Myrick announced it was time to collect their artwork. She asked the students to lay their papier-mâché sculptures on the windowsills, over the radiators, to dry.

Later that day, Miss Myrick told her, "Sam, I want you to stay after school today. I want to call in Miss Lee."

Miss Lee was the principal, a large woman who wore black, high-top shoes that clomped on the hardwood floors. Calling in Miss Lee usually meant a student was in trouble.

Miss Lee was harder on the boys than the girls. She used a wooden paddle on the boys when they were naughty, but she never hit the girls. Aside from her punitive measures, Miss Lee was usually kind. Every day, she brought into the schoolyard a heavy, foot-high bronze school bell and offered someone the chance to ring it to alert the others that lunch or recess was over. Kids fought over the privilege of being chosen to run around the grounds, ringing the heavy bell with its metal clapper. Still, she was the principal, and being privately noticed by her didn't bode well for most students.

Oh, no, Samantha thought. I did something wrong, and now I'll be punished. She spent the afternoon trying very hard not to cry.

When the three o'clock bell rang, the children shuffled out, but Miss Myrick said, "Remember, Samantha. I want you to stay. We have something to show Miss Lee."

Miss Myrick briefly left the room.

Sam trembled when she heard Miss Lee clomping

down the hall from her office two doors down. She watched Miss Lee's formidable form enter the classroom while Miss Myrick, behind her, shut the door. Cringing, Sam expected a lecture or some scolding. She would probably be kept for after-school detention, which was Miss Lee's preferred method of punishing a female student.

As the two women stood above her, Sam waited for the hammer to fall. She was surprised when Miss Myrick pointed to the windowsill at the papier-mâché sculptures made by the first graders.

"Miss Lee, I want you to know that Samantha made the best papier-mâché in the room!"

What? Sam was shocked. The assignment was to create an animal. She hadn't followed the assignment, because she didn't know what animal to make. She wasn't really sure what she did. She just tried her best to work with the paper and glue. Her relief was so great, she almost cried. Finally, she smiled.

Miss Lee hugged her.

"I'll write your mother a note about why you're late coming home from school," Miss Myrick said. "I know that on most days you walk home, and your mother might worry."

She wrote a note, signed it, and handed it to Sam, who took off running. She ran all the way home to hand her mother the note. Her short-lived accomplishment was never noticed by her father, though, and her distracted mother barely smiled.

The Death of Leta Boyd Stringer

Through much of Sam's childhood, her mother was homesick for California. Miriam was born in Mississippi, but her father, Rowan Stringer, moved the entire family to California during the Great Depression when Miriam was a child of only six. The Stringers, along with the Boyds and hordes of other poor people from the South, went west looking for work.

After almost a decade in California, most of which Rowan spent as a roaming Pentecostal minister, he moved his immediate family, minus Miriam's two older sisters who were established and had jobs, back to Mississippi. Miriam's parents and siblings never returned, either.

Although Rowan, Leta, and their four youngest children returned to Mississippi, they didn't remain for long. Most of the family eventually returned to California in yet another migration, but Miriam stayed in Mississippi. Rather than head back west, she married Benjamin Warren Cook shortly before she turned eighteen.

Ben had been awarded a scholarship to attend an accounting school in Chicago. He was valedictorian of his senior class at Paulding High School, but his family wouldn't let him accept the scholarship due to his father's fear of the North.

"Where's Chicago, boy?" he asked Ben. "If it's north of

Mississippi, you can't go."

Instead, Ben attended a one-year business school in Laurel, Mississippi, thirty miles from his home. Laurel was the county seat of what was once the "Free and Sovereign State of Jones," a county that reunited with the Union during the Civil War. The town was notable as the home of Leontyne Price, the African American opera singer. It was also famous for the notorious case of Willie McGee, a Black man who was electrocuted in the Laurel courthouse in 1951.

McGee was convicted of raping a White woman, Willette Hawkins, after Willette accused him of the crime. McGee claimed they were having an affair. The evidence produced during the trial was convoluted, anecdotal, and confusing. During the six years of Willie McGee's imprisonment, letters requesting his acquittal and pardon went all the way to the president of the United States from such notables as William Faulkner and Albert Einstein. Bella Abzug, a social activist and women's rights leader, was a young attorney at the time. In one of her first civil rights cases, she represented McGee's appeals all the way to the Supreme Court. His case, however, ended typically, with his execution rather than his exoneration, no matter the cause célèbre.

In the late 1930s, more than a decade prior to McGee's execution, Sam's father rented a room in Laurel from his mother Lola's cousin, Ida Mae Easterling, who happened to attend the church where Miriam's father, Rowan Stringer, was pastoring, having recently returned from California. Cousin Ida Mae took Ben to church with her, and there he met Miriam Stringer, a slim, stylish girl, who wore her long dark hair in a chignon, pulled back from her face at the sides with combs. Within a year, they were married. Ben was almost twenty-three, while Miriam was one month shy of eighteen. They entered their union on June 17, 1939.

Young Miriam had been offered an art scholarship to the Minneapolis School of Art, but her father, much like Ben's father, wouldn't allow her to attend.

"Girls should not be educated," he said, "especially not

anywhere in the North."

If Ben and Miriam had been allowed to follow their dreams, Samantha would never have been born.

When Miriam's family return to California, she visited as often as she could — which wasn't often. After Sam turned seven years old, those trips to California had a sad note, because her grandmother, Leta Stringer, died of esophageal cancer.

Her sickness came on suddenly. When Leta and Rowan, as well as Leta's sister with her family of four from Virginia, had visited them in Mississippi in August of that year, all was well. Upon receiving the news in October, 1949, that Leta was dying, Miriam hurriedly left for California, taking her first plane ride and leaving her husband and children behind for six weeks.

Sam always remembered that terrible six-week period. Those weeks were the first time in her life that her mother had been away. Her beautiful and playful mother meant everything to her. Sam didn't attend daycare, preschool, or kindergarten, so for four and a half years, Miriam and Sam were sole partners and playmates.

Before Lilah Jo was born, Sam's days were filled with Mama. They walked and talked all day. Mama read to her constantly and taught her everything she knew. Side by side, they played in the sandbox and on the swing set out back. Because the family had only one car, they walked everywhere. They went all over town, visiting her mother's friends, going to doctors' appointments, and on shopping excursions. On the rare occasions when Miriam had the car, they drove.

In the summer, Miriam took Sam to swimming lessons at the local college pool at the edge of town. Later, she taught Sam to cook and allowed her to make fudge any time she wanted, as long as they had enough cocoa and sugar. Mama did it all. After Lilah Jo was born, Miriam became the center of the world for the two little girls, not just for one.

Sam remembered an incident involving an iron swing

set in the backyard of the duplex. It had two swings and a set of monkey bars that could be detached. If the bars weren't being used, they often lay on the ground, where they eventually rusted.

Sam and Lilah Jo's next-door neighbor, Mrs. Lipscomb, lived in a beige stucco house with red trim. Sam always thought that house was made of stucco, because the Lipscombs were stuck up. No one from that family ever came outside except Ricky, the grandson. No one knew if Ricky lived there full time or just visited a lot, but on weekends he always seemed to want to play in Sam, Lilah Jo, and Oogie's backyard.

Ricky Lipscomb was very mean, and Lilah Jo, who was young and tiny, couldn't defend herself against a larger, more aggressive, bullying boy. Whenever they played, Ricky lifted a monkey bar and hit Lilah Jo over the head, sending her screaming into the house to tell her mother.

One day when that happened, Miriam marched out the back door, picked up a monkey bar, and hit Ricky hard in the back with it.

"Now you know how it feels!" she snapped.

Ricky screamed and ran to the stucco house. Sam didn't recall playing with Ricky after that day.

Miriam was protector, playmate, and friend to her daughters. Without her, they wouldn't have been able to pound a nail or change a light bulb. Their dad couldn't seem to do those chores. As a bookkeeper at a local car dealership, he was more interested in numbers and money than building or maintenance. When he needed a sandbox for his daughters, rather than building it himself, he hired Black laborers to build it for him. What would they do without Mama?

With Miriam suddenly gone to California, Sam was alone with her dad, who had to work, and her little sister, who was only two and a half and would never remember that time. It was the loneliest Sam had ever been. Without Miriam, the house was lifeless. Sam cried herself to sleep every night, thinking her mother would never return. The family needed help.

Mamaw Lola came to the house, and Sam hated her. The last time she had seen Lola was during the horrible burning incident, when Sam had saved her life. Sam still shivered when she recalled that day, remembering her grandmother screaming in the dirt beside the embers that burned the soles of her feet.

Though Lola was barely fifty years old, she seemed ancient. The large, anxious woman replaced Sam's playful, sweet mama, and she terrified Sam with her fearfulness and odd ways.

Since Sam was a little older, she was even more afraid of Mamaw Cook than before. In Jasper, Lola's strangeness matched the surroundings. In Hattiesburg, she contrasted in a frightening way with Sam's normal life.

Stone-faced and stoic, Lola made it clear that her priorities were household duties. She spent her days changing the baby and washing cloth diapers in the bathtub with lye soap, as Miriam did. She hung them on the clothesline in the backyard as their mother did, too, along with all the other clothes, sheets, and towels. She cooked Southern meals of pork or roasts along with sides of home-canned crowder peas and fried corn or rice with grease gravy and cornbread at each meal. While Miriam was away, they ate an endless supply of canned preserves, "termaters," mustard or collard greens, and eggs for breakfast and supper. Lola worked daily to keep the four-room duplex swept and dusted. She said little, but when she spoke to Sam, it was to tell her to eat, get dressed, or answer the door, as Lola was too fearful of strangers to answer it herself. Every day, Sam trudged the seven blocks home from Camp School, knowing that Lola would be silently waiting for her.

Thanks to Sam's busy second-grade social life, however, she didn't have to spend all her time with her strange grandmother. Outside of school hours, she played with Cissie as much as possible and enjoyed herself during school, too. She loved her second-grade teacher, Miss Daniel, who kept her lovely red hair pinned in a bun. During art class, which was held in the gymnasium, fresh-faced Miss Daniel would tell her students, "Color as thick as butter!" Samantha always wished they could color outside the lines, which was strictly against Miss Daniel's rules, but for a few hours each day, Sam was able to forget her mother's abandonment and the grandmother she had a hard time loving.

In the mornings, Ben quickly shaved, dressed, and walked to work. He usually didn't kiss his daughters or say goodbye. Sam knew he was sad that Miriam was gone. A strange woman, his mother, was in the house, keeping them, but he never spoke of it with the girls. It was as if it wasn't happening.

Evenings were spent listening to the radio before bed. Every single night, Sam cried herself to sleep in a cot in her parents' room, where her father slept alone in the bed beside her. Lola took over Sam's bed, so she could tend to Lilah Jo during the night in the girls' bedroom. Sam was convinced her playful mama would never return. That was the new norm, an empty house filled only with the sound her father snoring and her grandmother clomping around in her old-fashioned, lace-up black shoes.

Beyond the household chores, the strange, silent woman did nothing Sam's mama did. She didn't read to Sam or play with her outside. She made sure Sam was dressed, but she didn't even comb her blonde curls.

During those six weeks, Lola sent Sam down to the corner to Cissie's house every morning before school. Cissie's mother, Audri, would have just finished plaiting Cissie's long, light-brown pigtails and tying them with a bow. When Sam arrived, it was her turn. Audri tried to comb and style Sam's shorter curls.

Frustrated, Audri said, "I just can't do it like your mother would." She finished by clamping a plaid or solid-colored bow atop Sam's head.

Audri's attempts at styling Sam's curls fell flat on the day second-grade pictures were taken. Sam's hairstyles never lasted past noon, and the photographs were taken after lunch and recess. Samantha's long hair drooped, looking unkempt and uncurled. The bow on top hung off to one side. In the photo, Sam looked exactly how she felt with her mother gone—depressed. Even her beloved school life, which provided an escape from Mamaw Lola, was becoming tainted by her mother's disappearance. She felt only resentment for her grandmother, rather than her usual joy at playing and learning.

Her mother called only once during her absence of six weeks in Bakersfield, California. Sam hovered nearby, while Ben did all the talking. Mama didn't ask to speak with Sam, and her dad didn't think to ask if she wanted to talk to her mother.

After six long weeks, Miriam returned on an airplane similar to the one that took her away to California. Ben's boss, Mr. Barron, paid for the round-trip ticket from New Orleans to Los Angeles and back. Mr. Barron, who owned both their first and second apartments, was always a source of extra support for the family.

Miriam told Sam about the transcendence of flying for the first time through the clear blue sky, above the clouds, where all worldly pain was so far below it felt like she'd never know it again. Of course, the loss of pain was only temporary. Three days after reuniting with her daughters, Miriam received the news that her mother had died. Mr. Barron offered to buy another ticket for Miriam to go back for the funeral, but she declined, being pragmatic rather than sentimental.

Sam's joy at her mother's return was brief. Miriam became grief-stricken and tearful. For several weeks, Sam's mother cried at least once a day. Any playfulness Sam had looked forward to vanished. Even so, Sam was glad to have her mother back and to know that her strange old grandmother from Jasper County was gone.

Thankfully, Miriam wasn't alone in her grief. Tall, skinny Great Aunt Tera, Leta's sister, arrived soon after Leta's death.

She came from her home in McComb, Mississippi, to stay with Miriam for a week. Samantha had many fond memories of Aunt Tera, the only member of her mom's family who lived nearby when Sam grew up.

Back when Leta's family, the Boyds, moved three generations from Carter's Creek, Mississippi, to the San Joaquin Valley in California, Tera, the Boyd's oldest daughter, was already promised to marry Hiram Norman, who had a good job as a railroad engineer on the Illinois Central.

Tera Boyd Norman was the only sibling among the six Boyd children to stay in Mississippi. Sam's grandfather, Rowan Divan Stringer, wanted to marry Tera, not Leta, but she wouldn't hear of it. Besides, she was already betrothed to Hiram.

Tera clearly made the better choice. She and her two daughters, Mary and Marjorie, had a good life because of Hiram's engineering job, even though he wasn't home much. Hiram died young, and, from that point forward, Tera lived on his railroad pension. Her two daughters walked to work downtown, one at a bank, the other at a gas company. Marjorie, the eldest of the two daughters, married in her forties and had two children, despite the fact that she had a form of epilepsy. After childbirth, she would never again hold a job.

Soon after Aunt Tera's visit to Hattiesburg in the wake of Leta's death, Sam was invited to spend a week with the Norman family in McComb over the summer. McComb was approximately seventy miles west of Hattiesburg, on US Interstate 98. In the 1940s, it was a thriving railroad town, a maintenance hub for the Illinois Central cargo and passenger trains, which ran from New Orleans to Chicago. Later, in the 1960s, it had some of the worst racial episodes of the Civil Rights era.

Sam rode the seventy miles alone on the bus, dressed smartly in a new dress with a dark-blue, dotted-Swiss skirt and a white top. She wore a white hat, white shoes, a shoulder purse, and carried a new cardboard suitcase. At the tender age of eight, she looked like a seasoned traveler. She sat up front near the driver, whom Ben had asked to keep an eye on her, and she watched the scenery pass.

It was Saturday. As they drove through Tylertown, twenty miles from McComb, Sam was astonished and baffled by the scene out the window. Black farmers in wagons shopped on the main street of town! Sam had seen such wagons downtown at Bay Springs, near where Lola lived, but never in her own town.

As was the custom in Hattiesburg, and later at her family's new home in Poplarville, Blacks weren't allowed to shop on the main street, so the sight of Black people shopping freely on Main Street shocked her. Apparently, Tylertown was more progressive — or at least different — than the rest of Mississippi. That small hamlet allowed its Black citizens one day a week, Saturday, to park their wagons and trucks on Main Street. All the White folks stayed home that day unless they owned a shop.

At age eight, Sam thought, This is all too strange. This must be a Negro town, and I've never heard of it. Many years later, Sam met her future husband at Baylor University, and he came from Tylertown. Since Tylertown was in a more agrarian area than where Sam grew up, she initially thought he was a real hick in whom she didn't have the least bit of interest. The next year, she fell in love with him, and six years later, they married.

Tylertown was supposedly more liberal, but sadly, it wasn't less racist. The citizens of Tylertown, being farmers, were simply more practical about their segregation. Unlike the White farmers who avoided town on Saturdays, the Black farmers couldn't come to town during the week, because they were tending their land.

Once Sam arrived in McComb, she had a fabulous time with Great Aunt Tera, her second cousins, who were young adults, and her new friend, Cecilia.

Cecilia lived next door to Aunt Tera, and she and Sam were the same age. Cecilia was adopted by an older couple who let her do whatever she wanted. Sam was a tad envious, but admiringly so, as she watched Cecilia make her own tuna fish lunch, drink as many Cokes as she wanted, and ride her bike all the way up to the McComb cemetery and down the hills to the edge of town, totaling a mile. The girls took turns on the bike while they roamed the town. At lunch, they headed over to see Aunt Tera, who was always waiting with a fabulous Southern meal. Tera's daughters, two "single girls," walked home from work to join them.

The five women often enjoyed a feast of fried chicken, fried yellow squash, fried okra, fried eggplant, and cornbread and fresh tomatoes. Sam and Cecilia loved all the vegetables.

After eating as much as they could, they topped off the spread with homemade chocolate pie or banana pudding made from scratch. For supper, as was typical in the Deep South, they ate leftovers or cereal.

Sam visited Great Aunt Tera often over the next several summers. She delighted in hanging out with her older, adult cousins. In the evenings, they taught her evil things, like how to play cards or how to paint her fingernails and toenails. Sam swung on the porch swing with Cecilia, read comic books, and gorged on delicious food.

Once, when Sam was eleven, she made an appointment to have her tonsils out, because she wanted to "have them out when her friend did." Afterward, she felt miserable with a sore throat.

Aunt Tera called and said, "Let her come for a week and get well here. I'll take care of her and pamper her."

Ben promptly drove Sam to McComb. For an entire week, she slept in Aunt Tera's room and was thoroughly pampered. She woke every morning to a piping hot bowl of Cream of Wheat. After eating, she could sleep as late as she wished. During the day, she gorged on puddings and other soft, delightful foods that Aunt Tera prepared.

Sam's visits with Aunt Tera's family also made Miriam

happy. With most of her family in California, Miriam found it especially important that the Cooks maintain relationships with family members living nearby in Mississippi or Louisiana. Miriam relied on Ben's family as a substitute for hers, which was another antagonizing aspect of their marriage.

Ben didn't care much for his own family and was estranged from his brother Elton, whom he didn't get along with. He and Miriam bickered about it. When it came to family closeness, just as religion, the couple disagreed.

Sometimes, Miriam made the long, hot, sticky drive down near Grand Isle, Louisiana, to stay with Elton's wife for a few nights. Elton may or may not have been home during those visits, depending on whether it was his time to work offshore. Her brother-in-law and his family moved regularly. Over the years, Miriam and her daughters visited them in Grand Isle, Morgan City, Houma, and several south Louisiana towns. Ben never came with them.

Although Miriam attempted to feel close to real family, for the most part, the Cooks found family among their community, instead. Long-time friends like Ann Jordan, the nurse who delivered Samantha, along with neighbors, work friends, and church members comprised a surrogate family they could truly rely on.

Fishing with the Cooks

Ben Cook was a fisherman at heart. When he was a boy in the deep woods country, his family sometimes didn't have anything to eat unless he and his brother set trotlines in the creek at night, hoping to snag a few catfish by the following morning. Benjamin Warren, named for his grandfathers, Benjamin Cook and Warren Morgan, learned to fish when the men of his family took the boys on camping trips by the creek to fish and cook out for the whole weekend. Later, after he married, Ben taught Miriam how to fish, and she loved it. It was one of the few hobbies Ben and Miriam truly enjoyed doing together. So in addition to their visits to Jasper County, the Cooks spent many vacations fishing.

When Samantha was eight years old, Ben and Miriam invested in a small fishing camp near Vancleave, on land leased from "Old Man Lucas," a corpulent soul who lived on the property permanently in a screened-porch house. "The Camp" was down on the Singing River, which flowing into the Pascagoula River, which then empties into the Gulf of Mexico.

During these family drives through the southern backwoods of Mississippi, Sam stared out the window just as she did on the long cross-country train rides to California. Back in those days, when families traveled, children weren't given things to keep them occupied. Staring out the window was good for the child's soul, giving them time to daydream and think about life, as they allowed the scenery to pass through their minds and hearts.

Driving east along the two lane Gulf Coast Road, US 98, they passed Biloxi, arrived at Ocean Springs, then cut north on Shell Road. When the pavement ran out, they bumped along dirt roads and oyster shell paths until finally, several hours after leaving Hattiesburg, they pulled into "The Camp."

The Camp was a tiny house trailer with a porch around all four sides. The porch had cots and bunk beds on three sides. The whole thing was in the middle of a thick, dense swamp of brown, muddy water filled with water oaks and swamp red maples, not to mention snakes. In later years, when Ben owned his own business, he sent some of his Black employees ahead to mow around the camp and kill any snakes they found—black snakes, cottonmouths, coral snakes, water moccasins. But the first time the Cooks visited "The Camp," they arrived unprepared for what they would encounter.

They all hopped out of the car and headed in to check the area. On the way down the hill to the pier, Sam and Lilah Jo saw a huge swing hooked to a larger-than-life oak. They couldn't wait to swing out over the water, though they weren't allowed to jump in. The Singing River was dangerous as well as disgusting, filled with alligators and trash.

Sam and Lilah Jo went inside the cabin with Miriam, set down their bags, and unpacked groceries. Miriam unwrapped a package of bacon for the girls, then went outside to help Ben, as the girls baited crab lines with pork. They strung the bait along the edge of the shore, knowing they would feast on boiled crabs that night.

While Ben was unloading the car and the girls were baiting crab lines, they heard a scream. They ran outside and saw Miriam on the dirt path leading to the cabin, hacking at something on the ground with a hoe. A long black snake was dead in front of her, cut into pieces. The normally reticent Miriam wore a satisfied smile.

After Sam and Lilah Jo had spent several hours playing and Ben had netted some crabs, they returned to the cabin only to find two more snakes eating back the head and tail of the dead snake on the path. Miriam grabbed the hoe and made quick work of the two new snakes. Those were the first, though not the last, of the snakes that Miriam or Ben killed during their years in the backwoods Mississippi bayou.

In addition to snakes, there were spiders, including many daddy longlegs. Sam and Lilah Jo killed a dozen or so before bed, after they pulled the plastic sheeting off the cots and arranged the sheets before crawling in and going to sleep. Thankfully, they never found any snakes inside the house, though there were plenty of holes the reptiles could have come through.

~

As a child, Sam enjoyed fishing with her family. During their early trips to Jasper County, Sam loved walking with her dad down to Nuakfuppa Creek to check on the trotlines. They couldn't see the creek from Mamaw's house, but it was always on their minds as they sat on the porch telling fishing stories. In one early photograph, Samantha is four years old. Dressed in pastel-colored overalls with the staple white rag around her head, she stretches tall to hold up a long line of catfish that had been caught overnight.

As Sam grew older, however, she learned that she preferred to stay indoors reading rather than going fishing outdoors with her dad, and she eventually came to dread their trips to the Camp, with its lack of modern amenities. There was a toilet on the back porch, but no lavatory. To wash hands or hair, they used the tiny kitchen sink, and the only bathing option was a three-sided, cold, tin shower situated outside.

While Sam grew to loathe the trips because there was

no TV, radio, or telephone, Lilah Jo still loved the fishing camp. She always liked animals and running around in the dirt, while Sam preferred to stay clean and be inside with the comforts of home.

Unfortunately for Sam, Ben and Miriam considered those trips the height of relaxation. Sam didn't understand. They had to eat from cans and throw all their trash into the river, from sanitary napkins to paper and tins. They watched alligators try to eat it all.

To assuage her boredom, trash-eating alligators notwithstanding, Samantha brought books or comic books. She stayed in the trailer house or sat on the screened porch, mostly away from mosquitoes, chiggers, spiders, and all the other creepies that crawled or flew.

"Samantha," Miriam chastised, "why don't you go out and fish for crab? You're not being adventuresome at all."

Miriam wished Sam enjoyed those trips more. She asked Sam why she didn't roam the woods like the others kids, but Sam wasn't interested in getting poison ivy, or, worse, bitten by a snake. She and Lilah Jo had enough poison ivy to last their entire lives. Over the summers, Miriam lanced many leg boils. They kept Epsom salts in the cabin, so they could soak their itchy skin.

One evening, when Ben came in from fishing, Miriam whispered to him that Sam wasn't having a good time. "Ben, I wish she'd try something new. I want her to have good memories of our vacations."

Ben walked over to Sam and sat down. "Hey, dropped lips. Why don't you come with me in the morning?"

Sam, a sullen preteen, squinted at him. Her dad hardly ever asked her to do anything special with him, so the offer was hard to refuse—but four o'clock was awfully early.

The next morning, Sam stretched under one of Mamaw Lola's quilts where she'd been sleeping warm and comfy. Ben came over to tousle her hair.

"Get up, girl."

She slouched out of bed, pulling on shorts and a T-shirt

Once they were in the dinghy, Ben said, "We're heading clear out to the front."

That meant down the river, through the bayous, and all the way into the Gulf to fish for flounder and other saltwater fish.

It was a long day. At first it was fine in the dark, but, once the sun came up, it was hotter than Sam could bear. The sun and smell of seawater seared her nose and churned her stomach. Rolling water stretched for miles. Under the hot sun, her eyes felt filmy, and the air was so thick, Sam thought she could see wavy lines floating in front of her. Without warning, she threw up over the side of the boat.

Still feeling dizzy, she slumped across the seat until Ben finally turned the boat around. When they got back, Sam stomped into the cabin and slammed the door, crawled under the quilt, and listened to her parents murmur about her.

The following day, the rest of the family prepared to go onto the water.

"Let Sam sleep and read," Ben said. "Leave her here alone. She won't wake up until we're back."

But Sam didn't want to be left alone, either. She'd never been taught what to do if she saw a snake. Sitting alone in the cabin that day while her family went off without her, she felt afraid and wished she had a friend to keep her company.

Florida Serendipity

Ben Cook and Miriam Stringer both grew up landlocked— Ben in Jasper County, and Miriam in Mississippi, Louisiana, and the San Joaquin Valley, where there was so little water her family had to share the same liquid for bathing in the big galvanized tubs. Despite Ben's love for the water, he didn't see the ocean until after he married Miriam — and that was merely the Mississippi Gulf Coast, which was mostly ugly and brown, with little surf to speak of. Still, he loved swimming in the saltwater of the Gulf.

Miriam, on the other hand, had already seen the Gulf as a child, since her family sometimes went to see her grandfather, Moses Stringer, at the Jefferson Davis Confederate Soldiers' Home in the seaside town of Biloxi, Mississippi. Beauvoir, Davis's former estate, had been transformed into a veterans' home when his widow sold it to the Mississippi Division of the United Sons of Confederate Veterans around the turn of the century.

Once or twice a year, Ben, who loved car racing, took a trip with a carful of other young men, including his mentor, J. O. Barron, to the races in either Chicago or Daytona Beach, Florida. In 1949, on the way back from Daytona, he took a new route that had just opened through the Florida Panhandle. All along US Highway 98, he saw beaches lined with crystalline sand made from quartz. Once upon a time, the beautiful, sparkling sand had been deposited there by glaciers from the Appalachian Mountains. That sand is the whitest in the world, whiter than the beaches in the Caribbean. After admiring the sand, Ben couldn't believe his eyes when he saw that the water was totally clear. When the sun hit the water, it reflected the most beautiful blues, greens, and aquamarines.

During that fateful drive through Florida in the spring of 1949, Ben was so excited about that gorgeous beach that he determined to take his whole family there the following summer. He did that twice in 1950, when Samantha was seven and Lilah Jo was three. The Cooks stayed in one of the two motels between Fort Walton and Panama City, the Frangista Beach Inn. They had a basement room without air-conditioning, though it was a breezy, by-the-sea apartment. The motel was owned by a Greek couple, John and Ruth Nitsos, who claimed the water was the most similar to the Mediterranean Sea that they could find in the United States

Eventually, the Cooks graduated to staying twice a year at the Capri by the Sea Motel. The nearby beach had a high cliff of white sand leading down to the water. Once or twice on those vacations, they splurged and stayed in what were then very nice three-room cabins near Destin Harbor at Silver Beach Cottages. They always made the trip just after school let out, then again on Labor Day weekend. After their Labor Day getaways, Samantha always dreaded coming back home to begin the routine of school the next day.

Those were the best and most private of the Cook family vacations. They usually lasted only three or four days, and everyone enjoyed their time at the gorgeous beach. During those trips, Ben was the cook. The rooms had kitchenettes, and he rose early to swim for an hour alone at six o'clock, floating on his back, staring skyward. He then returned to the motel, woke the family, and cooked a huge breakfast of eggs, bacon, biscuits, and grits.

After breakfast, the girls went swimming and played in

the sand. There was no sunscreen, and Ben was careful that his family didn't get sunburned. He insisted they return to the room by eleven o'clock. They usually slept or read, had sandwiches for lunch, and went outside again around four. They stayed at the beach for several hours before returning to the motel, where Ben would grill steaks on the lawn and cooked potatoes inside. For one night on each vacation, they drove to restaurants in Panama City, forty miles away, for spaghetti or soft-shell crabs.

Ben helped Lilah Jo jump waves. During the first of those trips, when Lilah Jo was three years old, she disappeared for a time when she decided to take a walk by herself. She was about a mile down the beach when Miriam spotted and ran after her.

Other than that, all was peaceful. They built many sand castles and watched the waves wash them out. Every night, Ben took the family for a walk along the shore. He always said, "Just think. The ocean waves beat like this on every shore of the world. It's hard to imagine."

For one entire week during the second or third year, he skipped Destin and took them all the way to Daytona, on the Atlantic Ocean. When Lilah Jo saw them drive past the Panhandle beach, the one they were accustomed to, she screamed and got a fever, because they weren't going to "the beach." Sam relished their time in Daytona, but the Atlantic waves were too rough for Lilah Jo, who mostly just played in the sand with Miriam.

Those trips to the Florida Panhandle continued for many years. After Ben bought the Ford car dealership in Poplarville, he became so accustomed to recommending his customers to Capri by the Sea that he received a discount from the Capri's owner, Mr. Black.

In 1950, that entire stretch of beach contained only two motels and one set of cottages, which Sam loved more than any place they stayed. The entire beach eventually filled with condominiums of different sizes. Even the Capri by the Sea Motel was eventually renamed Capri by the Gulf and transformed into small condominiums.

One can no longer see the Gulf from the road when driving along scenic Highway 98, nor the offshoot road farther east, 30-A. Developers filled the space with all kinds of buildings, large and small homes, condos, shopping centers, and even town centers containing newly minted town names. Over the years, the Cook family grew attached to that little stretch of the Gulf Coast, and they were disappointed to watch it grow and change through commercial development.

The End of Fourth Avenue

When Sam was eight, the Cook family moved four blocks away to a large garage apartment on Hardy Street. They lived upstairs, entering the apartment through a screen porch, past a swing Sam loved and played on frequently. The majority of the rooms were upstairs, but they also had a room on the first floor that could be entered only by way of an outside door. This room adjoining the garage had an old couch that Mamaw Lola slept on when she visited, as well as an old piano. There was never a rug in that room, so Sam and Lilah Jo would practice piano with their feet planted on the cold, gray, linoleum floor.

The new apartment belonged to Ben's boss, Mr. Barron, just as their duplex had. Ben was the bookkeeper at Barron's auto dealership, Barron Motors. Mr. Barron originally built the garage apartment for his wife seven years earlier. By then, J. O., as his friends called him, was sent off to war, leaving his wife, Susie, alone with Little Susie to care for. Originally from Atlanta and a debutante in her younger years, Big Susie eventually became an alcoholic.

The garage apartment, though nothing to brag about, was more comfortable for a family of four than the old duplex. Sam's family certainly wasn't wealthy—they were still in the lower middle class—but even so, little did Sam know that they had privilege by just being White in the deeply segregated South.

Although the move didn't represent a change in the family's economic status, their new location meant that Sam and Lilah Jo no longer had to drink the occasional glass of milkwater at supper. On Fourth Avenue, the grocery where they shopped was five blocks away, almost downtown. If Miriam learned late in the day that there was very little milk in the jar in the fridge, then milkwater became the treat for their evening supper.

In the garage apartment, though, they were only half a block from the Triangle, a very small market where three streets came together in a triangle. Miriam was able to send Sam there to get milk at the last minute. Sam loved the Triangle, where she could look at all the candies, popsicles, and ice cream bars before finally buying a quart of milk for her mother. If she had a few of her own coins, she bought herself a treat and hid it from the rest of the family.

Around the same time, Miriam began to allow Sam to go alone to the huge downtown library on the bus. Sam's family owned no books except the Bible and a *How and Why* set of books for children, but with weekly trips to library, Sam had plenty to read. She would come home with her arms stacked with six or eight mystery novels or orange-colored biographies, read them all in a week, and return the next Saturday for another armful. She loved walking up the formidable circular cement steps into the stately yellow brick building, which made her feel important and smart. Although she didn't think about it at the time, those visits were a privilege afforded only to White children. In segregated Hattiesburg, Blacks weren't allowed in the library.

Despite these newfound joys, the move from Fourth Avenue marked the end of Sam's Eden. No more would she walk to school with Cissie each day, nor would she enjoy the beauty of Pine Street, with its tall oaks and azaleas. In Sam's memory, it always seemed like springtime on Pine

Street, with temperate, cool, pristine weather all year round. Now, Sam walked alone down a stark, ugly alley, crossing yards that were never as beautiful as those on Pine Street. Sometimes on the way home, she stopped to play in the ditch by the side of the alley with various friends who were mostly tomboys, unlike herself. Mostly, though, she preferred being inside, reading Nancy Drew or The Hardy Boys.

Very close to Sam's apartment across busy Hardy Street was Oak Lawn Cemetery, the largest and oldest cemetery in the small city and the final resting place of many of the town's founders. A half block beyond those hundreds of graves, on the other side of the graveyard, Sam's Brownie troop met at her friend Alice's house. Wearing her light-brown uniform and brown felt beanie pinned to her hair with a bobby pin, Samantha often walked across the cemetery to Alice's house, and sometimes, after the Scout meeting, the girls played on the cemetery grounds.

One afternoon, as Sam headed back home through the old cemetery after Brownies, she saw someone who would forever be emblazoned in her memory as "The Lady in Black." Sam first encountered her among the gray tombstones and green grass in a long black dress that nearly touched the ground, black shoes, and black gloves. A black hat decorated with black feathers rested atop her head, and a black, polka-dot veil covered her face.

Frozen in fear, Samantha stared at the woman who strolled through the cemetery, seemingly as comfortably as in her own living room. Sam watched as she enter a mausoleum, stooping to go inside. Eight-year-old Sam was both fearful and curious.

The following week, Sam set off to find the Lady in Black at the same mausoleum, this time with Alice and the other girls from Brownies in tow. The troop of girls sneaked across the cemetery, darting in and out among the graves, and peered at the mausoleum from a few feet away, remaining hidden behind tombstones.

They saw the woman inside, sitting beside a stack

of magazines. The girls watched, as the woman had a conversation with a phantom family. They remained silent, as if playing hide-and-go-seek, hearing only their small hearts beating and the sound of their own breath.

"I heard her husband and child are buried there," Alice whispered.

"She's crazy," Brenda said.

"I heard she talks to ghosts," Linda hissed.

The woman came to the cemetery by bus each morning and stayed all day, or so the girls thought.

One Saturday morning, Sam waited at the bus stop near her home and the cemetery. She planned to go downtown to her beloved yellow brick library. The Lady in Black suddenly walked up beside her, as if appearing from thin air, and Sam started shaking. She almost ran home to the garage apartment to Mama, but the pull of the library was too strong. Nothing could come between Samantha and her books. There was no turning back.

The tall, thin woman looked down at Samantha through her veil, staring spookily. Her eyes glittered, and Sam thought her breath might freeze through her veil as she spoke.

She smiled. "You're a pretty little girl. I had a little girl who looked just like you, but she died. I don't have her any longer, but I come here every day and talk to her."

Sam didn't smile or speak. *I'm not your little girl,* she thought. *I'm not dead.*

When the bus came, Samantha was glad she could step up on the steep steps and go. She watched through the window as the bus pulled away, taking her away from the eerie woman who waited for another bus to take her home, where no one waited for her.

New Beginnings

Although Cissie and Samantha remained in the same Brownie troop, and their paths continued to cross, the move from Fourth Avenue marked the end of their close friendship. At first, after the Cooks moved, the girls visited each other. Cissie rode her bike to the garage apartment or Sam rode her bike to the grand mansion. But they ended up quarreling over who won the game of hopscotch on the sidewalk or how many acorns each could stomp on and crush. They fought about whether the devil lived under the cracks in the sidewalk and whether they would or should step on top of his residence. During one of those discussions, Cissie berated Sam's mother's Pentecostal religion.

"At least she could be a Baptist, like your dad!" Cissie shouted.

To Sam and her girlhood friends, religious beliefs were less important than where one went to church. Pentecostals didn't have the highest standing in Hattiesburg, as Cissie's comment made clear.

The religious tensions between the girls went both ways, however. Although Cissie's parents were Presbyterian and her grandmother, Joey, from New Orleans, was Catholic, Sam had the erroneous impression that Cissie was Episcopalian. One Sunday they went with their Brownie troop on "Visit

Churches Day" to the historic Episcopalian church on Pine Street, just down the boulevard from Cissie's house. Everything about the Episcopalian church was different from Sam's church. The stained-glass windows gave it a spooky, haunted feeling. The altar was filled with candles, and the elusive scent of incense filled the air. Instead of spontaneous praying, the congregants knelt on hard benches while reading prayers from a book. Sam wondered how they could see to read in the dark.

Miriam told Sam all those things were of the devil, but how could that be, Sam wondered, if he lived under the sidewalk cracks? If it really was of the devil, how did he get from the cracks into the candlelit Episcopalian church on Pine Street?

As Sam struggled to make sense of the devil and the different churches in Hattiesburg, she and Cissie seemed to sense that they didn't belong in each other's worlds anymore. Whenever Cissie got angry with Sam, she tried to manipulate her with the threat, "I'm going home!" She rode her bike one block away and looked to see if Sam was begging her to return. Worse, she would go to Sandra Toussaint's house across the street and ask Sandra to come out to play. Sandra, in her very fine clothes, always sided with Cissie in their group of three, a very bad number.

Sam never had Cissie to herself again after she moved four blocks away. It seemed an eternity from Cissie's big house. After a while, Sam stopped asking her to come over. They drifted apart, but time eventually repaired their childhood rupture. Forty years later, when Sam lived in Houston and Cissie lived in Connecticut, she wrote to Sam.

The letter informed Sam that Audri, Cissie's mother, was moving. Aylen, Cissie's grandmother, and her husband, Charles, had passed away, and Audri could no longer keep up the big house alone. Audri was selling the grand mansion on Pine Street and moving into a townhouse on the outskirts of the city. Cissie asked Sam if she'd take a trip to Mississippi to help her remove her old dolls from the attic. She hoped to reminisce with Samantha about their childhood days of playing with the dolls in her many playhouses.

Unfortunately, Sam was ill and couldn't go. From her home in Houston, she remembered Aylen's poppy garden and Cissie's playhouses, including the pretend ones they made outside with walls of pine straw. She thought of the attic, where they played with dolls, and the long walks to school along the beautiful oak-lined streets. When an opportunity arrives and is missed, it leaves forever—but endings often contain the seeds of a new beginning.

Sam deeply regretted not helping Cissie with the move, but they stayed in touch afterward. The two old friends found they were still compatible, with similar views on spirituality, reading, and sightseeing. They continued their newfound friendship until, much later in life, they met for a trip to Charleston, South Carolina, and Sam eventually visited Cissie's lovely home on a lake in Brevard, North Carolina.

Boy Trouble

From her third-grade teacher, Sam learned that life wouldn't always be fun and games. In Miss Grace's classroom, the students were forced to sit in perfectly linear rows, which felt draconian compared to Miss Myrick's classroom next door, where they sat at little oblong tables.

Stepping out of line was never allowed in Miss Grace's class. The students and teacher were utterly silent during her early morning announcements, after which the group learned to stand in synchronicity to proclaim allegiance to the American flag with the rest of the school. This ritual was led by the principal, Miss Lee, over the loud-speaker, blaring into every class. When the loudspeaker fell silent, Miss Grace made them say the Lord's Prayer. If a student didn't know the invocation, Miss Grace required the child to write it out many times until he or she could recite the prayer properly. Luckily, Sam already knew it from church.

Miss Grace's strictness didn't change the attitude of the devil-may-care boys sitting in the back rows, who attempted to wriggle out of the rules by flying paper airplanes. Miss Grace's quick eye always caught them. Her desk drawer was full of paper airplanes. Along with the confiscation came a desk change for the criminal, creating a constant rotation of boys from the back to the front of the class.

Samantha had been taught to follow the rules from a young age, thanks to attending two churches and bearing the responsibilities that followed from being the eldest child. She was not only a smart pupil with excellent spelling skills, but also a well-behaved one. She must have caught Miss Grace's favor, for Miss Grace made her tutor some of the other girls — never the boys — in the hallway on spelling words they missed on a test. Some children felt insulted to be coached by a fellow student.

The students learned not only proper phonics but also parts of speech and how to diagram sentences. Proper spelling was imperative, and Sam's tutees needed to catch up. She tried hard not to lord it over them, but it never mattered. They always seemed to resent her.

Sulky girls skulked into the hallway with an attitude of, "Who do you think you are?" Even one of her own playmates, the daughter of her mother's friend, was downright rude and refused to look at the word or its spelling.

One afternoon after trying hard to be a good student and spelling coach to her peers, Samantha left school to go home for lunch, feeling downtrodden and misunderstood. She trudged heavily down the steps of the school. When she reached the far edge of the school grounds, Billy, a fifth-grade boy, walked up beside her holding a brown paper sack.

Billy, who seemed very tall, didn't say a word, as he fell in step with her. Sam barely reached his shoulders. She wondered why he carried a sack lunch and left school to eat it. Why wasn't he eating in the cafeteria? A moment later, he thrust the bag toward her, silently urging her to take it. She looked up into his face, then took the bag and nodded. Why was he giving her his lunch? He ran back to the school.

When Sam got home, her mother stirred something on the stove.

"Hi, Mama," Sam said, running into her bedroom before her mother turned around.

"Sam, come in here and eat lunch!" Miriam called.

"I have to go to the bathroom!" she called back.

Once safely in her room, she unrolled the brown paper sack and peered inside. Suddenly, the morning's stress melted away. Her present from Billy was a bag full of round, individually wrapped pieces of bubble gum. There must have been a hundred of them. Knowing her mother would find it, she stuffed the bag into her middle clothes drawer toward the back, then ran into the kitchen.

Her happiness at having a bag of gum, however, was short-lived. The next day, as Sam left for lunch, Billy was waiting for her again. Her heart sped up and she wondered, What does he want? Will he ask me to be his girlfriend?

Frightened, she didn't know what to say. As he fell in step with her, he quickly handed her a bag and ran away down a side street.

That went on for weeks. Once or twice a week, Billy showed up as Sam left for lunch and handed her a bag of gum. She never knew what to say, and he never said a word. He just handed her the bag. She wished she could stay and eat lunch at school to avoid the encounter, but her father would never let her stay at school for lunch just to avoid a boy. The price of lunch was twenty-five cents, and her dad, the numbers man and a would-be accountant, quickly realized that added up to $1.25 a week or $5 a month. That much money would buy a lot of groceries.

She wanted the gum, but she didn't want to be Billy's girlfriend, which she felt certain was his intention. One afternoon, as Sam arrived home from school, she sneaked into her bedroom to deposit yet another bag of gum. On top of her dresser were all the contraband bags of gum. Heart pounding, she set down the new bag and walked into the kitchen, staring at the floor, as Miriam looked at her.

"I discovered your little secret," Miriam said.

Sam immediately told her the story of Billy and the gum, speaking so rapidly, she could barely get the words out. "I don't know what to do about it, Mama! Can't I just stay at school and eat lunch there?"

A slow smile spread across Miriam's face, and Sam was

instantly furious.

"Is he your boyfriend now? I bet so!" She laughed as if that were the most hilarious thing in the world.

"No!" Samantha shouted. "He's not my boyfriend!"

"Samantha, you can just tell him you don't want any more of it. You don't need to give back the gum." Miriam was calm, not understanding her child's distress.

"You don't understand! Can I eat lunch at school?"

The saga of Billy and the bubble gum ended with little fanfare when he stopped giving her the gum of his own accord.

~

Sam entered the fourth grade, and her new teacher, Miss Lenore, was a looming presence in the classroom. Miss Lenore was a large, Germanic woman, big-boned and tall, with black-dyed hair. She only liked the girls in her class and hated the boys, often locking them in the cloakroom, an enormous closet used as a passageway leading to the class beside them, where fourth-grade students with lower scores were taught. The cloakroom also housed coats, boots, and books. Boys were sent there for up to half a day for being naughty.

Miss Lenore was a proponent of math and wouldn't graduate any child from her class until he or she learned everything she taught for their grade level in mathematics. She drilled endlessly on division, addition, multiplication, and fractions.

Samantha had hated math before but found it easier to understand Miss Lenore's teaching than other teachers.

One afternoon, when Sam was answering math facts for Miss Lenore, she felt a tiny pop beside her ear.

"Ouch!" she muttered quietly, turning to stare angrily at David Hinton. Her boy troubles clearly hadn't ended with Billy and the bubble gum.

He shot yet another dried pea toward her right ear with

his cut-off bamboo peashooter. As Sam glared, he laughed at her. He was too quick for Miss Lenore, who never caught him in the act. He didn't want to be imprisoned in the cloakroom, and he knew Sam wouldn't tattle on him. She had enough problems without reinforcing her classmates' impression that she was a goody two-shoes. She must endure.

Sam had known David for years. His mother taught Sam's Sunday school class at Ben's Baptist church. David and his four brothers lived with their single mother in an identical duplex on Fifth Avenue that was right behind the Cook's old duplex on Fourth. They played together a few times when they were younger, but David's clan of five boys, whose father deserted them, was too wild for her. She didn't see how David's mother, who worked in the lingerie department of Belk's in downtown Hattiesburg, survived. She raised those wild boys by herself and plugged on with an incredibly busy life that included teaching Sunday school and other church work.

Eventually, dealing with David and his peashooter turned out to be worthwhile. Many years later, when Sam began college in Texas, she was waiting outside in the Central Texas September heat in a registration line. Who should she encounter in the same line but David Hinton? He recognized her, though she didn't know him at first. When she realized, all she could remember was the sting of peas on the back of her neck. That day, however, David introduced Samantha to Ed, the young man from Tylertown, Mississippi, who would be her future husband. She supposed the pea shooting was worth it, and David was redeemed.

Curl Jane and Floor Nail

By the time Sam was nine years old, she and her sister both attended the First Assembly of God with their mother, no longer congregating at the Baptist church with their father. It had been a gradual transition. When Lilah Jo was born, Ben had tried taking both girls with him for a while, but he found he couldn't manage both of the children during church services, especially with one in diapers. He still took his Sam to church occasionally, though, even after Lilah Jo put a wrench into their regular routine.

The final straw came when Samantha was baptized. Miriam insisted Sam be baptized in the Assembly of God Church. In Pentecostalism, as in many Protestant denominations, children aren't baptized at birth, but only when they make an individual decision to follow Christ and declare that decision to the Church. Sam walked the aisle in response to the invitation and made it known she wanted to follow Christ. The next step was baptism.

Since their church building had no baptismal pool, the ceremony was conducted at a stagnant pond on a Sunday afternoon at four o'clock when Sam was eight years old. Ben refused to attend the baptism, but he finally realized just how insistent his wife was about her beliefs. He gave up and relinquished both little girls to accompany their mother to church.

Ben was one of many fathers in Miriam's church group whose wives considered their husbands "lost." Sam learned about being lost and saved during loud, scary sermons. As preachers screamed lessons about hell, damnation, and getting ready for the Second Coming of Christ, Samantha worried that her father was going to hell.

Those services, with their long, complicated, emotional altar calls, seemed to last forever, and Ben was often waiting outside in the car for his wife and daughters after church. The family had only one car, so Miriam and the girls often caught rides to the First Assembly Church, which was at the other end of town from their new house. Sometimes, they switched, and Ben caught a ride or walked. But since his church service ended at noon, and the Assembly services dismissed a bit later, he usually came to pick them up.

One Sunday morning, First Assembly was having a revival with a guest preacher. Revival services tended to last longer than their typical Sunday morning services, so when Sam, her mother, and Lilah Jo finally came outside at one o'clock in the afternoon, Ben had been waiting for almost an hour. He was furious. He'd been listening to the thundering sermon from outside. Annoyed by the content as well as the wait, he lost all patience, which he was short on to begin with.

Sam and her sister hustled into the back seat, sensing their father's anger. Miriam slid into the front seat and shut the door.

"Anyone in the world can get up there and scream like that!" Ben shouted.

Miriam was hurt that he insulted a speaker she enjoyed. "Not anyone can preach like she did!"

And so the bickering began. Sam sighed. It wouldn't be pretty at home that afternoon. Sundays at the Cook household were almost always one extreme or the other. Most Sundays were deathly quiet, but an argument over religion could shatter the silent household in a moment. Listening to her parents argue about religion made Sam feel sick.

Aside from the deafening silences or boisterous fights, they ate well every Sunday. Some mornings, Sam woke to the smell of chicken in spattering grease, to be eaten later that day. After a big dinner of fried chicken or pot roast, complete with sides of mashed potatoes, green beans from a can, and a homemade pie or cake for dessert, Sam's parents quietly rested in their bedroom—if they weren't fighting. Either way, Sundays were a dreaded part of Sam's week.

While Sundays at home were either boring or full of tension for Sam, she loved to spend the afternoon with her church friends, Flora Nell and Carol Jean. Their father, Pete, was also "lost," although he was more "lost" than Ben. Rather than opt to attend a different church, Pete spent Sundays drinking beer and arguing with his wife, Ida. It was a similar scene, but it was easier to stomach when it wasn't Sam's parents.

"Floor Nail" and "Curl Jane," as their mother drawled their names, lived near the church. Sam believed those to be their real names. Flora Nell was two years older than Sam. Carol Jean was a year younger. The three girls played happily together, while Pete and Ida either fought or didn't speak. Perhaps they were fighting over religion, too. Since Pete never spoke to her, and Ida was too busy cooking, Sam never knew what really antagonized the two. Either way, it didn't stop Ida from going to bed with Pete all afternoon. Sam was almost certainly as much of a distraction for the sisters as they were for her.

Sunday dinner fare at Floor Nail and Curl Jane's was similar to what they ate at Sam's house. When Ida cooked, she used every pot and pan in the kitchen to make a main course of delicious meat and several vegetable sides. After eating, the girls were required to wash all the dishes before they were allowed to play. There was no dishwasher, of course.

Floor Nail, the oldest, was in charge of washing the dishes. Curl Jane and Sam dried and put them away. Since every pot and pan had been used, it was an extraordinary task for the girls. All that work took them until three o'clock or three thirty, given that they often didn't get out of church until afternoon or one due to the typical long-windedness of their preacher or guest speakers.

The girls were expected back at First Assembly for children's night church at six, so they had two hours, three if they were lucky, to play before they had to come in.

During those Mississippi Sunday afternoons, they entertained themselves with various activities. Some days, they enjoyed a stroll to the store to buy a popsicle. Sometimes, they played in ditches or with Carol Jane's dolls. Other times, they found more kids outside and played tag or chase or hide-and-seek. It was always more fun than going inside to the ticking tomb bomb of the household.

Sometimes, Sundays at home could be fun, too—on the rare occasion when Sam's parents weren't arguing about religion or when they kept quiet for the sake of not arguing. If Sam wasn't spending the afternoon with Flora Nell and Carol Jane, sometimes her dad suggested a ride to see friends. On those days, they stopped at a drive-in and got an ice cream cone or a hamburger and Coke. Ben didn't like ice cream or hamburgers, but it gave Miriam a break from cooking supper. Those must have been the days when Ben felt especially affable toward his wife.

~

Luckily, there was more to church life than bellowing pastors and arguing parents. Miriam and her friends attended the Women's Missionary Society, which met once a month at night to pray and take up money for the missionaries in the field, though most of the discussion was about the Second Coming of Jesus. One of the older women always used to say, "Every noise I hear in the house now, I think maybe it's the Lord returning." Sam thought she must be crazy. Even so, Sam always looked forward to Saturday mornings in winter when the same women met in the new church kitchen to cook hot tamales, which they sold in order to donate the proceeds to the missionaries.

Sam enjoyed watching all the eclectic characters as wonderful smells and steam filled the air. The delicious tamales were made from scratch. Beef or pork filling bubbled on the stoves. Women hand-mixed the corn mush, and the tamales were boiled and wrapped in corn shucks. She had never had any Mexican food before, or any foreign food, except spaghetti. She thought tamales were totally exotic and assumed without doubt that no one but those women could prepare them. They all seemed so talented and full of adventure to make and sell such tasty, enticing food. Even in her later years, eating a warm, savory tamale in winter would bring back those fond memories

Christmastime

When Christmas came, Samantha always looked forward to her mother's homemade candies. Every year, she proudly delivered divinities and bits of fudge to her teachers on paper Christmas plates wrapped in red or green cellophane and tied with a bow of homemade ribbon.

Even more than the candy, though, Sam enjoyed bringing her teachers home with her for a special Christmas lunch. Miriam collected Sam and Miss Lenore from school and brought them back to the house, where she prepared a meal that would normally be prepared only on Sunday afternoons. Sam felt proud as the air filled with the enticing smells of fried chicken, home-canned vegetables, rich iced tea, and the most delicious apple pie on earth. She could hardly wait. Miriam was a master pie chef, and apple was one of her best

Sam's father, Ben, loved Christmas. Like a child, he rattled the wrapped presents Miriam placed under the tree, guessing what they were and wondering if he couldn't open "just one."

Finally, on Christmas Eve, Miriam allowed him to open one gift, but they waited until Christmas morning for most of the celebration. He always took Miriam coffee in bed and made breakfast for the family, often waffles with strawberries. Then came Santa Claus and gifts.

When Sam was in first grade, some kids at school told her the truth about Santa. She didn't believe them and ran home to ask, "Mother it's not true, is it?"

Miriam's answer didn't comfort her. "Yes, it's true, but don't tell your little sister." Lilah Jo was just two years old.

That year, Sam felt there was nothing to live for at Christmas. Mamaw Lola was with them, and Sam had to sleep on a cot in the living room. The six-year-old cried herself to sleep saying, "There's nothing left. I might as well go ahead and die."

She had a very miserable Christmas that year, but she eventually found that Santa wasn't the only thing that made the holiday special. For instance, Christmastime was a time of connection for Samantha and her sister Lilah Jo. Normally, they had different interests. Sam was a bookworm, whereas Lilah Jo preferred spending time outdoors with friends down the street, playing in the ditch and searching for polliwogs or crawfish. But the holidays had a way of bringing them together.

Sam always remembered the Christmas when she was eight years old and Lilah Jo was four. They were given Terri Lee dolls. Those were expensive imitation china dolls made of plastic with delicately painted features consisting of wide-set eyes, pouty lips, and carefully styled hair. Sam's doll had pale, white-blonde hair, while Lilah Jo's was a brunette. The girls decided to switch dolls to match their own hair color. Both sisters kept their dolls as keepsakes through the years, and, eventually, they became collectors' items.

Their parents spent so much on the dolls that they couldn't afford the wardrobes to go with them, so while Mamaw Lola made quilts and little doll mattresses with the cotton she grew, Miriam spent much of that fall sewing an entire wardrobe for each doll, carefully copied from the catalog, and then hiding her sewing from her daughters. These doll clothes were intricately made and encompassed a full wardrobe, including bathing suits and wedding dresses.

Miriam was a decent seamstress and her creativity always came out at Christmastime.

When Sam was in fourth grade, Miss Lenore's class was assigned the task of performing the school's Christmas pageant. It would be held in the gymnasium, which also doubled as the auditorium. They practiced for months, starting right after school began in the fall. Practice took place on stage, which was really just a section at the far end of the auditorium. They performed multiple acts, including the nativity play and other short productions.

While Samantha and her classmates were carefully memorizing just about every Christmas carol that ever existed — "Silent Night," "Jingle Bells," "Hark! the Herald Angels Sing," "O Little Town of Bethlehem," "Rudolph the Red-Nosed Reindeer," and "Good King Wenceslas," among others — Miriam helped behind the scenes. She and Sam had a good laugh over the bags of chicken feathers Miriam used to construct angel wings for Sam's costume. The feathers came courtesy Mamaw Lola's white leghorn chickens, with material arranged along the back.

That same year, Ben surprised Miriam with three train tickets to California. He would stay in Hattiesburg, while Miriam and the girls made the long journey. It would be the first time since she married that Miriam would be able to spend Christmas with her family. Before departing, they bustled around the house packing. Miriam was in an especially good mood, but one thing weighed on her mind. "If only Mother were going to be there," she said morosely to Sam and Lilah Jo. It had only been a few years since Leta had passed, and perhaps Ben realized that, with Leta's death, his wife needed to spend more time with her family.

Sam was in a great mood, too. Miriam bought her a brand-new dress to wear on the trip. She put it on and twirled in front of the mirror, admiring herself. Her mother bought it because it would remain wrinkle-free on the two-day trip. Sam loved the orange skirt and gray jersey top. The dress, smartly trimmed in orange, made her feel grown up.

She was ready for anything.

As she admired her dress, she heard her parents talking in the next room, the tone had changed. Sam always knew when a fight was brewing. She slowly crept into the hall to listen.

"You didn't book a bedroom?" Miriam sounded mildly exasperated but not surprised.

"Sorry," Ben said. "I didn't get to it in time."

Sam waited for her mother's explosion, but it didn't come. After a brief silence, Miriam bustled out of the bedroom and called, "Girls, are you packed? Let me check your suitcases."

The following morning was hectic with getting dressed, eating breakfast, and loading the luggage into the trunk of the Ford. Ben seemed impatient, Miriam was frazzled, and the girls couldn't wait to get on the train to New Orleans.

Miriam and the girls had coach seats, not their usual private room. Miriam sat at the window, Sam on the aisle, and Lilah Jo between them. Across the aisle from Samantha sat a Frenchwoman from New Orleans. She wore lots of perfume and makeup, and her henna-colored hair was pinned in a chignon atop her head. Sam had never seen anyone like her before. In conversation with Sam, she often asked, "Oui?"

Sam thought that meant, "Is that right?" so she kept chatting, trying to understand the woman's accent. She later learned the woman meant exactly what Sam thought and was actually listening to her. It seemed that neither one could understand much of what the other said, but Sam loved talking to her and hoped to see her on the train back to Mississippi, as well.

The return trip, however, was even more memorable. Miriam and the girls headed to the train station, expecting another long journey in coach seats. When they arrived at the train station in Los Angeles, though, they had a shock. The Sunset Limited train to New Orleans was crowded with twice as many people as the last time. The train company accidentally sold all the seats on the trip twice! People piled up in the rows and stood in every available spot. Children splayed out on the train floor because there wasn't enough space. It was hot, hectic, and chaotic. The entire two days seemed filled with anger, exhaustion, fighting, and cursing. If anyone got up from a seat for any reason, it would be taken by the time he or she returned. The staff was forced to open the private bedrooms to allow people to sleep. Women and girls were in one room, men and boys in another.

Sam and Lilah Jo slept on the couch in the restroom with their mother for a few hours. Sam was mostly perturbed because she couldn't look out the window, which was her favorite part of traveling by train. To add to their discomfort, the train ran out of food because they had double the expected orders.

After two exhausting days, they arrived in Mississippi. The trip had made Miriam tired and cranky, and by the time she got off the train, she was utterly spent. Ben knew nothing of what happened. He was happy to see them, and he became irritable when Miriam brushed him off. They fought on the way home, and Ben, in his anger, hit the accelerator.

As he sped through a small town, he was pulled over by a cop, who admonished him for reckless driving.

"You might not care for your own life, but you could at least care for the lives of your children," he said.

That Christmas trip wasn't what any of them had expected.

~

Several years later, the Cooks had a Christmas adventure with fewer mishaps. Ben asked a woman who worked in his office to wrap six boxes for Miriam, one inside the other. All were empty but the last, which held a note:

> *Tonight you will spend the night beneath the bright lights of a big city, and see wonderful things, and have a special dinner you won't have to cook.*

"What does this mean?" Miriam asked.

"Pack your bags for one night," he replied.

Not until the family was in the car did Ben say they were spending the night in New Orleans. They had gone before, just not on Christmas Day with its miracle of lights.

The family made the eighty-mile trip, arriving in the city just before dark. They went straight to Saint Charles Avenue to see the bright mansions, resplendent with glimmering lights. Sam looked on with wonder as they made their way down the wide sidewalks, past iron fences.

That night, they stayed in a room Ben had reserved at the Hilton Hotel near the New Orleans airport. Next door was a Polynesian restaurant., which fascinated Miriam and the girls. They had never been to such a restaurant. They loved the food, and Ben joked with the waitress by asking, "Don't you have any cornbread?"

The waitress, who was from East Asia, had never heard of cornbread.

That trip to New Orleans was a favorite Christmas memory Sam held close to her heart, a special time when the family was together in harmony and happiness.

The Platform

The Cook family's next trip to the California desert came in the summer between Sam's fourth- and fifth-grade years. Miriam and Ben had been fighting more than usual, and Miriam, ready for a break from her husband, decided to take the girls to see her family.

On the way, Miriam seemed cranky and exhausted. Sam was old enough to have some insight into her mother's moods and guessed she was thinking about how exhausting her marriage was.

Ben was trying to buy a car dealership in Poplarville, Mississippi. He worked late nights and came home exhausted. Snappish, angry, and cranky about most things, he picked fights with his wife. Miriam could barely stand to be in the same room with him some days, and Sam was sick of the tension between her parents.

As the train headed west, it made one of its usual stops in Yuma, Arizona. The antsy girls were excited during the train ride, and Miriam wanted them to leave her alone for a few minutes so she could rest.

"Girls, come here!"

They were crowding each other by the window, both trying to see out.

Miriam dug in her purse and took out six one-dollar bills. Giving them spending money was an extravagance they usually couldn't afford. She handed each girl three dollars.

"Here. Go buy something pretty and make sure you're back before the train leaves."

Miriam trusted Samantha with Lilah Jo. She had a tendency to run off but would usually stayed close to her older sister.

Sam, feeling very grown up, grabbed her four-year-old sister's hand as they skipped merrily off the train. It felt good to be trusted with Lilah Jo, and Miriam often praised Sam for being mature for her age.

Alongside the train platform at Yuma was a stretch of tables occupied by Indian women selling wares. Sam, who loved looking at the silver and turquoise jewelry, spent a lot of time trying on various pieces until she finally settled on a beautiful bracelet emblazoned with arrows and a turquoise heart. She spent two dollars on it. Many years later, she had it appraised at approximately $150. At the time, two dollars seemed an extravagance. Next, for one dollar, she bought a turquoise cross necklace.

As Lilah Jo paid for her own piece of silver jewelry, two large black male arms suddenly surrounded both girls. The man scooped them up into his strong limbs, and started running. Before Samantha had time to become frightened, she realized he was running toward their train as it pulled away from the platform. They hopped aboard as the train slowly moved away. For several minutes, the man searched the cars until he located Miriam.

"Lady, what's wrong with you?" he demanded. "Don't you love your children? What would you have done if the train left without them?"

His tone was angry and scolding, as if talking to a child. Sam had never heard a Black man address a White woman that way.

Miriam, passive as always, murmured, "I'm so very tired, and my older daughter is very mature for her age."

Sam didn't feel mature in that moment, and she wondered what would have happened if she and Lilah Jo had been left on the platform.

Final Days in Hattiesburg

Before Sam turned ten, the family moved again, packing up the garage apartment they lived in for only one year. The Cooks were no longer renting. Sam's parents had bought a small, redbrick home in a working-class neighborhood in Hattiesburg, where the houses all looked alike. It seemed obvious they were constructed simultaneously by one builder

For Sam, it was a lonely neighborhood. Though she was glad her family finally had their own house, there were no friends nearby for her to play with. Lilah Jo had a friend in the house next door who was older than Sam, but she was mentally challenged and therefore better suited as a playmate for Lilah Jo.

Luckily, Sam was still a Girl Scout, so she got to see her friends once a week at their troop meetings. On Saturdays, the band of six or eight girls roamed the town. They frequented a park with a zoo near Sam's house, and the girls might spend the entire day unaccounted for. There were no cell phones, so their parents never knew where they were.

When Sam was alone, she found ways to keep herself occupied. Their new home was half a block from the Jewish synagogue, which occupied an entire block, and Sam often skated or rode her bike around the building.

On Saturdays when Sam wasn't out with her friends,

she continued to frequent the public library downtown. She rode the bus there, spent half a day, and checked out seven books. By the time the following Saturday arrived, it was time to return the books and check out seven more.

Miriam had warned Sam never to get in the car with a stranger. But one day, a woman stopped Sam on the way to the library and said, "I know your mother told you not to ride with strangers, but I'm going right to the downtown library, where you must be going with your books. Would you ride with me?"

Sam got in the car, and the woman took an odd route. As they drove past Sam's house, which wasn't on the way to the library, Sam thought, *She'll murder me, and I'll never see my home or family again.*

Ultimately, however, the woman did take Sam to the library. She never told her mother about the incident, but it put such a fright into Sam that she remembered it for the rest of her life.

~

At the end of fifth grade, Miriam persuaded Ben that Samantha should be allowed to go to Girl Scout camp for two whole weeks. They had never been able to afford to send her before. The Cook family planned to move from Hattiesburg to Poplarville, and Miriam wanted Sam to have one last fling with her Hattiesburg friends before they left town.

That June, Samantha headed off to Citronelle, Alabama, in the back of Charles Goodrich's pickup truck with her old friend Cissie and six other girls. The ride was a blast, with the wind in their hair the whole way. The girls laughed and sang during the entire ninety-minute drive to camp.

When they arrived, they learned that camp wouldn't be all fun and games. There was a very strict schedule, no sweets were allowed, and if a girl disobeyed a camp counselor, she would be sent home.

Despite those rigid rules, the girls had a tremendous

amount of fun. They stayed up until the wee hours, whispering in the light from their flashlights. They ate toothpaste for its sweet taste, went outside in the middle of the night to walk to the bathhouse, and slept on the top bunk. They sneaked around wearing lipstick or painting their nails, which was strictly forbidden. While camping out in the woods with their sheets and blankets, they toasted pieces of dough on sticks over an open fire. The doughboys, as they were called, filled with butter and jelly, were the only treats the girls were allowed during the entire two weeks.

When the two weeks were up, they returned home the same way they'd arrived — in the back of Charles's pickup — marking the end of Sam's last big adventure with her childhood friends from Hattiesburg.

~

Sam prayed every night that they wouldn't have to move. She tried to control her fears, but the move was inevitable. She knew that. Her father had been driving eighty miles round trip every day since Christmas, when he purchased an auto dealership in Poplarville, forty miles away. Sam felt it might as well have been a million miles.

The family waited until the new school year to move, so Sam could finish the year in Hattiesburg. Miriam made sure Sam could finish elementary school and begin junior high in Poplarville. They also used that time to sell their house, which they'd lived in for less than two years. Sam hated the thought of leaving the one house they could truly call home.

Part Three
Poplarville

A New Town and a New School

The new rental house in Poplarville didn't feel like home to Sam. She missed her old house in Hattiesburg. Though they only lived there a short time, it was the first place they could truly call their own. Sam wished they didn't have to leave, but, eventually, the time came for the movers to pack up their things. She watched the men toss her belongings into boxes while she waited for her parents to drive her away from her beloved home. It was August 1953, and the Cooks departed Hattiesburg for the forty-mile drive south on Highway 11, the same highway that ran in front of Cissie's large house in Hattiesburg.

In Poplarville, they arrived at a house that sat on a huge two-acre lot with pecan trees in the back and rented for fifty dollars a month. Without any subflooring, it was cold in the winter and hot in the summer. They used space heaters to stay warm in the colder months, and during the summer, they ran the attic fan and kept the windows open. Even so, the "cooler air" wasn't cool. Nighttime temperatures were still in the nineties. Some nights, the hot air blew across Sam's body, leaving her drenched in sweat. Between the heat and the gaping hole in her bedroom floor, sometimes Sam didn't sleep the entire night. She worried that a rat or a snake would crawl in, like at Mamaw Lola's house, not the

111

mention spiders or other bugs. She often wondered why her mother couldn't have at least bought a two-dollar throw rug to cover the hole.

The one good thing about her new bedroom was that she finally had it to herself — sort of. While Sam no longer shared a room with her little sister, her new room opened onto a back storage porch with a clothes closet, washing machine, and food freezer, which made for a steady flow of foot traffic through Sam's private space.

With money they didn't have, the house could've been more beautiful, if only her mother had stripped the peeling wallpaper and repainted. If she had chicly decorated the two sides of the open front porch, the house would have been cute. If her father had taken the time to manicure the lawn, the house would have become a home.

When it came to spending, Ben had more long-term plans. All the extra cash he earned from his business was used to buy a lot in another part of town for them to build a better house later.

~

When the Cook family left Hattiesburg, they also left the Assembly of God Church. Just before they moved to Poplarville, Samantha and Lilah Jo had been playing on the swing set at their old church's outdoor playground when Sam overheard her mother talking to another parishioner. It was late afternoon, and Miriam was saying her final goodbyes to a friend.

"Miriam, don't let your children get that Baptist stuff in their heads," the woman said. "It's so bad, and it's not like what we teach."

"Oh, I plan to teach them myself," Miriam replied. "We won't go to the Baptist church."

But sometimes life doesn't go according to plan. In the new town, they had only three churches to choose from: Baptist, Methodist, and a Presbyterian church that met only once a month.Miriam realized that in a town of twelve hundred, one of the better places to meet people and make friends was at church, and that church had to be the Baptist church. In Poplarville, for the first time in her married life, Miriam sat beside her husband on Sunday mornings, and their daughters became members of the Baptist Church from then on.

Coincidentally, the Baptist minister's wife had been the daughter of an Assembly of God minister. The couple, knowing about Miriam's former denomination, welcomed her and her daughters by sharing that information with the congregation and welcoming them to the new church. They understood Samantha was already baptized in the Assembly Church, and later, Lilah Jo was baptized in the Baptist Church.

Having the opportunity to switch churches was a relief for Sam. While they awaited the move to Poplarville, Sam began reading a series of religious books, written by a woman from the Assembly of God denomination, expounding the importance of accepting Christ as one's savior. Failure to do that, the books claimed, would result in a fatal accident or tragedy, making a second chance at salvation impossible. Sam despised the woman in her mother's church who had loaned her the terrible books.

"Give them back to the woman," Sam said. "I don't want them!"

Sam didn't believe in the kind of God the books described, a God who would send someone straight to hell just because she didn't accept Him on a particular night in church. At ten, Sam knew those books were terrible for a child's psyche. She knew fear wasn't the best way to come to God. She spent her whole life understanding that.

Miriam's fundamentalism held firm, however, as did that of her family in California. When they were adults, Sam's sister told her that when they visited their California relatives, Lilah Jo thought God must live in the trees there, or perhaps the clouds. She always thought they crossed into another world when they crossed the state line. The family there discussed God in the most terrifying way, and Lilah Jo was filled with fear. One dark night, when Lilah Jo was seven, she ran into the middle of the street because their mother scolded her that "God sees everything you do." She wanted to hide from His eyes. Perhaps if she ran from the house into the darkness, He couldn't see her so well.

Sam didn't like the God talk among her family, but she was glad to have a family, and she wasn't frightened. She didn't believe everything the others said, anyway. Then and always, she went her own way.

~

While the family's church life was made somewhat better by the move, the same could not be said for school. Sam's new class at her new school was made up of half six-graders and half fifth-graders. All of her classmates seemed far behind her. Sam didn't understand it. All the lessons taught by her teacher, Mrs. Ford, covered material she already knew.

Sam desperately missed her fifth-grade teacher, Miss Golding. In Miss Golding's class, the lessons were interpersonal and cushioned with music. They spent part of each day singing camp-style rounds like "John Jacob Jingleheimer Schmidt" or "Dona Nobis Pacem" or "Kumbaya," which kept the students relaxed and happy to learn.

Aptly named, Miss Golding had a personality that shone as bright as her short red hair. A music major at the teachers' college, she had a gift for keeping the class under control. All the students loved her, and her musical talents were certainly part of what kept the children in good spirits all day. They felt lucky to be in her class rather than the class next door, where the children yelled all day.

While Miss Golding's class was disciplined and loving, Sam's new class in Poplarville was dull and boring, and there was no singing. During the first six weeks of school, Sam learned that Mrs. Ford's husband had recently passed away, and her son had died in a car crash. She must have been having a rough time. But Sam earned Mrs. Ford's favor, being the bright student she always was, so she decided to stay after class one day to request a favor from her teacher.

As the other students hurried from the class, Sam asked, "Mrs. Ford, do you think we could sing in class sometimes? In my fifth-grade class last year, we sang all the time. It really made the day much better."

"Oh, that! I forgot. Yes, we do sing. We sing on Friday afternoons at 2:30 until the bell rings at 3:00." She pointed to the corner of the room. "We sing out of those old orange songbooks up there in the closet. They have nice patriotic songs."

Sam grimaced. *Singing just once a week? How awful. And only at certain times? We sang anytime and all the time in Miss Golding's class last year.*

Back in Hattiesburg, Miss Golding wasn't Sam's only music teacher. There was another teacher, Miss Steadman, the "floating" music teacher who always arrived unannounced. Miss Steadman visited all the White primary schools in Hattiesburg, and the children always looked forward to her seemingly impetuous timing.

Carrying a pitch pipe, Miss Steadman was like the Pied Piper in a gathered Parisian skirt. When she arrived, the next thirty minutes became a magical break in the monotonous days of reading in a circle, doing math problems on the blackboard, reading silently, or trying to stay awake. She got the children to follow her immediately. She taught them *Do, Re, Mi,* and the rest of the scales, along with many other songs. Sam loved looking at her long hair, which she wore in buns of a variety of shapes. She was the embodiment of magic and grace.

There was no one like Miss Steadman at Sam's new school.

When they sang in Mrs. Ford's room, it was ghastly. There were no rounds. No "Itsy Bitsy Spider" or "Kumbaya." It wasn't the fun-filled, happy singing she experienced in Hattiesburg with Miss Golding and Miss Steadman.

Standing straight-backed, the class droned in lifeless tones "America the Beautiful" and "My Country 'Tis of Thee." The kids hated it, and Sam wished she'd never brought it up.

~

During that difficult first year in Poplarville, Sam felt like an outcast. She made only one friend in her class, Tandra, who was another social misfit. She wasn't an outcast in the same way Samantha was, but they had the comfort of their mutual difference as they kept to themselves.

Word had it that Tandra, her sister Joan, and their mother moved in with their grandparents because their dad killed himself the previous year. Their mother secured a job as secretary to the county agent in his office downtown. As a working mother, she had no way to check on Tandra and Joan after school, and the old grandmother certainly didn't look after them at all.

Tandra's big sister Joan usually went home after school and often invited boys over or talked to them on the phone. Joan was beautiful and participated in county beauty contests, which she usually won. She wore dresses her mother made at night, hunched over the sewing machine in her bedroom after working in an office all day.

Sam saw pictures of the girls' father with his horse. Apparently, he was a brilliant horseman. Tandra inherited her love of horses from her deceased father, and she eventually owned one and boarded it on a farm in the country. She later lived on a boat and worked at NASA nearby. Tandra married, but sadly, Sam learned that her friend became an alcoholic later in life.

Tandra's family lived on Back Street in an old house with slanted linoleum floors. The girls and their mother usually occupied only two rooms (both bedrooms) in the house, as the front room was cold in the winter unless they lit the old gas heater, which was seldom.

Rather than go home to a cold, lonely house, Tandra roamed the town until she met her mother at her office at five o'clock. She loved to window shop or browse the clothing stores, admiring dresses, jeans, and shirts. Sometimes, she opted for a Cherry Coke at the drugstore, or she combed the dime store, looking for a little treat.

Befriending this autonomous and rejected preteen was irresistible to Samantha. She was drawn into Tandra's sphere of desolation, and while there, forgot her own family's rules. Time lost all meaning when Sam and Tandra were together. Forgetful of her mother's worries and lacking established rules on what time to be home from school, Samantha wandered the streets with Tandra, often for too long.

One fall afternoon, after too many indiscretions, Sam approached her block just after five o'clock. With the recent daylight savings time change, it was nearly dark. She recognized her mother's car coming down the block. It stopped surreptitiously at the corner, waiting for her to cross the street.

Sam knew she was in for it. Her mother had no switch, but she parked the car, got one, and switched Sam all the way down the block to their rented house.

~

Between a ramshackle home and a wearisome class, Samantha's sixth-grade year was difficult. Years later, after Sam was grown and married, Miriam confessed to her that her sixth-grade class was for kids who were close to failing. Samantha should never have been in that class, but, when they moved to Poplarville in August, the achievement tests had already been held the previous spring, and the advanced class was full.

Instead of telephoning, Miriam wrote to Camp School in Hattiesburg for Sam's achievement test scores, but the records didn't arrive soon enough. Only after school started and the classes were set for the year did Sam's test results arrived to prove her intelligence and verify that she belonged in the advanced class. Then, from seventh grade onward, students at all learning levels were mixed together.

Though Samantha finally made friends, her former love for school didn't return. It wasn't so much because she had other things on her mind. Boys alone weren't enough of a distraction to keep her from being academically minded. Rather, it was because school was easy, which made it boring.

Beginning in the seventh grade, Samantha's bright mind began to waste away, leaving behind her love of books and replacing them with comic books and fashion magazines. The same bright girl who regularly read biographies of famous women never visited the library in her new town. She didn't even know where it was until after she had already left town.

Talk of the Town

Poplarville, like most small towns, had its share of townsfolk who didn't exactly fit the stereotypes of Southern municipalities. Abnormalities included being a gay man or a single woman with a creative streak—not that anyone in town spoke openly about either of those things. They simply watched and whispered through the lens of curiosity and entertainment.

Every community on earth has its eccentrics, but Sam always supposed that in her town, with a population of just over a thousand, they were especially distinctive. For Samantha, they provided the perfect embellishment for the town's social fabric.

Mr. G lived downtown over his hardware shop. He was said to be "queer." Samantha didn't know what "gay" meant then, nor was the term used. She had the notion that queer meant more than simply strange, but she was never really sure.

Then there were the town spinsters. Not all of them behaved in the manner stereotypically attributed to their type.

Word always spread rapidly among the teenagers on Friday nights when Miss Flotile, a known alcoholic, along with her New Orleans boyfriend, raced up and down Main Street in his large, four-door convertible. The two of them loved to scream and rage, gunning the engine, as they raced up and down the street. Most likely, they were drunk, although the teens watching had no clue. It was more entertaining than anything else in town—certainly more exciting than the segregated movie theater downtown, where the movies shown were always old.

When Flotile and her beau terrorized the small-town streets, local law enforcement barely acknowledged them, only occasionally stopping the duo to warn them they'd better pipe down. Flotile's behavior was tolerated, in part, because her sister, Miss B, was much more respectable and actually acted like a spinster. Plus, the two came from an old family.

The sisters lived catty-corner across from Ben's Main Street car dealership in a Victorian mansion. Years later, after Miss B died, the house was torn down by her successors, and a gas station was built on the lot. Miss B supported her wild-living sister with multiple jobs. She was a piano and voice teacher, and she headed the choirs at the junior college, which the high-school students could join. For a while, she also directed the choir at the Cook family's Baptist church. Her high vibrato voice soared with a tremolo to high heaven when she sang solos from the Messiah during Christmas celebrations.

In Poplarville, Lilah Jo took piano lessons from Miss B. When she was six or seven years old, Lilah Jo was learning scales one afternoon in Miss B's living room. As they sang, "A, B, C, D—" they were interrupted by Miss Flotile, who began to rage and shout from the attic area where she lived, separate from the main part of the house. In her rage, she called Miss B every name on earth.

As Lilah Jo related it later, Miss B calmly said to her tiny, blonde student, "Just one moment, please." She went upstairs and scuffled with Miss Flotile in the attic, apparently locking her in. When Miss B returned, she didn't miss a beat nor bother to explain anything. She simply opened her mouth and sang, "EEEEE."

Lilah Jo had amazing musical talent. When Sam was eight years old and Lilah Jo was four, their parents purchased a piano for Sam to take lessons. Sam played with moderate ability, while Lilah Jo, at four, sat down and played songs from the radio and church without any lessons and was able to use both hands. She begged for lessons, and, because of her prodigious talent, she was allowed.

Back in Hattiesburg, both Cook girls were coached by Mrs. Harper. For their spring piano recital, Miriam made her daughters matching formal gowns, with taffeta ruffles over the shoulders and netted, gathered skirts covered in silver circles. Lilah Jo's was pink, while Sam's was mint green.

At the recital, Lilah Jo played each note perfectly. She memorized her presentation and performed flawlessly, playing "The Spinning Song." She was so tiny, she had to be lifted onto the piano stool. She couldn't even reach an octave with her hands. The crowd recognized and appreciated her talent, clapping and cheering for her at the end of her piece.

When Samantha played "Für Elise" by Beethoven, she sat down, nervous about her first recital and jealous of her sister's reception by the crowd. Partway through, she realized she couldn't remember anything but the first phrase. She played it repeatedly, then jumped up and ran from the stage, embarrassed at her failure.

Many years later, when Sam was in eleventh grade, she took voice lessons from Miss B in Poplarville and was in choirs at the high school and the junior college. That semester, Miss B tutored the high school students on the famous Verdi opera *La Traviata*. The class listened to the entire opera on tape, studying the libretto. They sang certain passages and solos. They even took the bus to New Orleans to see a live production of the Italian masterpiece. They bought the least expensive seats and sat in the top row of a building that would eventually become the Superdome.

Sam adored the experience. When the character Violetta was dying, Sam was so moved by the music that not only did she weep, but she felt the urge to jump off the balcony in solidarity with the poor soul succumbing to tuberculosis.

While Lilah Jo took piano lessons from Miss B,

Samantha took lessons from Miss I, the other piano teacher in town. Ivelle O'Donnell, like Miss B, studied music at The Cincinnati Conservatory, which later became the University of Cincinnati College-Conservatory of Music, one of the finest music conservatories in the country. Miss I also lived in a Victorian home, but she tore it down during the years that the Cooks lived in Poplarville. In its place she built a smaller, more modern brick ranch house.

Rather than teach much piano, Miss I preferred to talk about her boyfriends from New Orleans. Sam learned no more piano than she had from her first teacher in Hattiesburg, Mrs. Harper, who believed in telling young students to play something they could recognize right away. Sam never learned to play more than a few hymns exactly as they're written in the hymnbooks, without improvement, improvising, adding parts, or key changes. And she certainly never had the excitement of a piano lesson with someone like Miss Flotile locked in the attic.

Skiing with Spice

Sam became part of a clique of girls who were more interested in socializing than studying, though that group didn't include Spice Crawford, Sam's on-going "new best friend." Ben took Spice along on several Cook family vacations to Destin, Florida, where the two girls shared a passion for waterskiing. That special sport was something Ben spent a lot of time and trouble on just for them.

During one of those vacations, Ben hauled a small boat for the two girls all the way to Destin, so they could ski around and under the very long Destin bridge. For a long time, the Destin area was a peninsula. Up until 1936, one reached the eastern side only by ferry. Even after the great bridge was built, before Sam's times in the area, crossing into Destin felt like entering a new, exciting world.

Everyone knew the Destin water was clean and pure. Submerged neck-deep in the water, one could see the bottom. Where Sam learned to ski, on Lake Shelby out of Hattiesburg, was part of the army base, and they never had to worry about snakes that might be in other lakes or rivers in Mississippi.

While skiing, Sam and Spice were careful to avoid the light-colored water because that meant the area was shallow. If someone fell off skis there, they could easily hit the bottom, risking serious injury. Sam and Spice stayed in the dark waters, crossing ropes, dropping skis to slalom on one ski, and perform as many water tricks as they could. It was wonderful—heaven, freedom, and the most fun Sam could imagine.

When they returned to land and ventured back to their motel room, the hot sand squeaked with every footstep. Sam eventually learned that the shape of the quartz caused that characteristic sound. One side of each grain was flat and it squeaked as the flat side of a grain rubbed against the angular sides of other grains. The Destin sand, minus a few dark grains brought in with the developers' dirt, is still as white as sugar—and still squeaks underfoot.

The Cooks all thought their special vacation destination was extraordinary. The trips, however, also included family conflicts. One summer, they rented a cottage at "Silver Beach," the only set of cottages on the Destin strip, and more expensive than the very few motels. Sam discovered a wonderful indoor restaurant with three sides of glass offering views of the water. They served hamburgers all day.

On several occasions, she went there alone and said, "I want a hamburger. Charge it to our cottage." Eventually, the owner, Michel, called her dad to report the behavior and the bills. Ben told Sam very sternly never to order there again because it was too expensive. She had to eat with the family in the cottage.

Once while they stayed at the "Capri by the Sea," Sam and Spice spent a day's worth of quarters on Cokes and hot dogs at a kiosk on the local pier. Ben never knew about that.

One day, Spice and Sam went into the kiosk in wet bathing suits without towels, their hair and eyelashes dripping wet.

The man working the kiosk turned to Sam and asked, "How ld are you?"

"Twelve."

"Oh, my. What a beautiful specimen of womanhood you'll be."

Sam's face turned red. She would never live down that remark if Spice had anything to do with it. Her friend laughed and teased her for the rest of the trip, saying, "Oh, beautiful specimen of womanhood! Huh!"

High School Days

By the time Sam began her high school years in Poplarville, the Cook family had moved from their rental home into a new three-bedroom ranch house they built. The house was very basic, with minimal amenities and no special beauty. Ben had spent two years saving money for the move, but Sam was frankly disappointed by the results. She imagined a large, elegant home, not a cookie-cutter house with two bathrooms, a small den, a kitchen, and a dining room that was part of the living room. It stood gracelessly by itself on a one-acre lot in the south part of Poplarville, on the opposite side of town from their rental home.

Sam appreciated the built-in desk and bookshelves in her room. The desk would eventually become infused with poignant memories. She used that desk in junior high, high school, and later in college when she returned home one summer to take trigonometry and chemistry at Poplarville's junior college.

There was another perk to the Cooks' second home in Poplarville—it was next door to the town's community center, though this place was a privilege enjoyed by White residents only. When integration became the norm, the community center was torn down, and the pool where Sam spent many summers in her teenage years was destroyed by being filled with dirt.

The swimming pool was the salvation for Sam and her friends during the hot summer months. It usually opened to the public around one or two in the afternoon and didn't close until nine at night. It never occurred to Sam to wonder where the Black kids spent their summers.

At the pool, boys flirted with girls, dunked them, and held them underwater. The girls strutted around, often in two-piece bathing suits that revealed whatever parts of their bodies were allowed to be shown in the 1950s.

When Miriam was ready for Sam to come home and do chores, or if she thought Sam had been in the sun long enough, she walked over and called her to the fence, or she drove by and honked the car horn. Sam knew that meant she had to get going.

While Sam spent many summer afternoons at the pool, she spent almost all Friday nights, even during the school year, at dances at the community center. Ben always complained that the jitterbug music was so loud, he couldn't sleep on Friday nights, but he never barred Sam from attending. She loved to jitterbug and, if she liked a boy, dancing close — especially if it was Bobby, the junior college quarterback and her first serious emotional love attachment. A very good dancer, Bobby was eighteen, while Sam was only fifteen.

Hanging out with Sam at the community center were Spice and the sisters Joan and Tandra. Sam remained friends with the sisters, who were only eighteen months apart and separated by one grade. They hung out in the same circles. There was also their friend Darla and whichever boyfriends they had at the time.

Samantha pursued various boyfriends with vigor. She'd been boy crazy since junior high. When she liked a boy, she adored giving him gifts even when he gave her none. She loved shopping for men's clothing at the stores downtown, where she charged her purchases to her parents' account until her dad found out. One Christmas, she bought a lovely red sweater for her country boyfriend, Doug, and her mother made her take it back. It was for the best, because he didn't reciprocate her love. She fell for Doug when he played the guitar and sang "Blue Christmas." The night of Mardi Gras, she smooched with him all the way back on the bus from New Orleans, but he never paid her any attention after that.

Then, Bobby from Alabama became the love of Sam's young life when she was fifteen. She fell for him hard. He was the quarterback football star of the Pearl River County Junior College, and, to Sam's utter dismay and eventual heartbreak, she shared him with her best friend, Spice Smith. They were a triad, as Samantha thought of them. She wanted to be a couple, alone with only Bobby.

During the summer between Sam's fifteenth and sixteenth birthdays, Bobby dropped Sam for Spice without telling her and with no prior discussion. He went that summer to visit Alabama, his home, where he had lived before moving to Mississippi. Sam visited him once in Alabama when she traveled there for a college tour, and again near Asheville, North Carolina, where Bobby was working at Ridgecrest Baptist Assembly. He was cold to her during those visits. She didn't know that he and Spice were already writing letters.

When school reopened that fall, Sam watched Spice, her supposed friend, hanging on her ex-boyfriend. Samantha felt lonely and angry. Spice never talked to her about taking Bobby from her. The silence between them hung like thick fog that never dissipated.

It was for the best that neither of them stayed with Bobby permanently, although for several years, it seemed as though he had a good life. He became a quarterback star at a major Florida university and was nominated for All-American football quarterback. He married Miss Alabama from his home state, obtained a law license in Alabama, built a practice and was elected attorney general of the state — but his life went downhill after that.

He was convicted of seventeen counts of white-collar crime, including bribery, stealing, and extortion. He spent three years in federal prison with John Mitchell, the attorney general under President Richard Nixon, who was imprisoned for his part in Watergate.

After getting out of prison, Bob's law license was revoked, and he was no longer the attorney general of Alabama. His wife, who waited three years for him, was a schoolteacher and likely had to support them on her small salary. They had three children.

Prison hadn't done anything to change Bob's wily ways. He continued calling Sam long after she married, saying he wasn't guilty of his crimes, and she was the sweetest girl he knew. But if his words were true, why had he dropped her for Spice?

Despite what happened with Bobby, Sam and Spice continued their complicated relationship throughout high school. No matter their boy problems, they were still friends. In fact, they were often mistaken for sisters because they had the same dishwater-blonde hair, olive skin, and they tanned similarly in the summer. Both were slender, though Samantha was taller. Sam supposed it was easy to see why Bobby liked them both.

One difference between the two girls was that Spice was athletic, whereas Sam preferred to stay indoors and read. Years later, when they worked together at summer camp after their freshman year in college, Spice taught horseback riding and swimming, while Sam taught Bible and crafts. Spice remained active throughout her life. In later years, Sam had recurrent nightmares in which Spice did great things and went to great places, leaving Sam behind. Though they remained friends, their relationship would always be complicated.

~

Sam's troubles with Spice didn't end with their feud over Bobby. There was also the issue of Spice's mother, Suzy Crawford, who was aggravating and intimidating. She intervened in all their affairs. Most of those interventions were well-intended, but nonetheless unpleasant.

Suzy had a penchant for sarcasm, which she used as a defense mechanism. Her words could be piercing and hurtful. She also had little to do outside her home. She spent her days cooking, gardening, and playing bridge.

One of the reasons Sam and Spice remained entwined was that their parents were friends of a sort. Miriam and Suzy had a polite friendship in that Miriam didn't really care for Suzy but tolerated her due to their husbands' business relationship. Miriam felt intimidated by Suzy's money and upper-class habits. Miriam didn't usually dress up during the day, but when Suzy called and wanted to drop by, Miriam ran to change into a nice dress. She also quickly fixed her hair and put on lipstick.

Where the real relationship came into play, though, was through the girls' fathers. Ben bought his auto dealership from Spice's father, George Crawford, who didn't need to work. The Crawfords were wealthy and lived on George's inheritance. George's father, who came from New Orleans, was one of the original founders of Poplarville. He helped form the first bank, bought the Texaco station, the first Ford dealership in town, and large swathes of land. Then, oil wells were discovered on some of his property. Spice's father inherited all of that and passed it on to Spice, her brother, and their three cousins.

The Cooks and the Crawfords sometimes ate dinner together in the Crawford's large traditional dining room. Suzy was a good cook. For one such dinner, Sam walked to the Smiths' house after choir practice at school. She let herself in the front door, knowing she was expected. Her parents and sister would head over after her dad got off work.

"Mrs. Crawford," Sam called, "do you know where Spice is? Me and her were going to hang out before my parents came over."

Suzy looked at her sharply. "She and I, Samantha. I believe she is in my sewing room."

Sam burned with embarrassment at the grammar

correction. It always stung a little more coming from Spice's mother. The worst thing was, Sam knew better. Occasional bad grammar was a habit she picked up from her mother, who often said things like, "Me and so-and-so did that." Miriam's sophisticated manners never extended to perfecting her grammar.

Ashamed, Sam made her way to the sewing room. Suzy sewed two dresses a week for Spice in a gorgeous room that held multitudinous fabrics and sewing notions. The room was organized from top to bottom with drawers and cubbies, including a fold-down cabinet off the wall that held every imaginable color of thread.

Spice lay on the sewing room's day-bed, flipping through a magazine. She jumped up and held the magazine out with the pages open to a beautiful dress. "Samantha, look at this dress! Mother's going to make it for me. I was just picking out material."

Sam wished she had as many dresses as Spice. She was glad she hadn't worn a new one that day. Whenever Sam arrived at the Crawfords' with a either a new sweater from town or a new dress from her mother's sewing machine—which didn't have its own room—Suzy said loudly, "Oh, I thought you had a new dress last week. Where did this one come from? Let's see, is it bought or made? Did your mother line it with taffeta that way I do Spice's? Does it fit? Oh, there's a thread hanging out."

In addition to the many dresses her mother made, Spice had dresses purchased from the best stores in New Orleans. Shopping in New Orleans was one of the widely understood status symbols in Poplarville. The wealthy families traveled to New Orleans for finer goods, whereas the less well-off families shopped at the stores in town or drove to Hattiesburg.

When Sam's parents arrived that night with Lilah Jo, they all went into the dining room. Suzy bustled around the table, adding dishes and heading back to the kitchen for requests. It was clear she was in one of her moods. Everyone felt uncomfortable as Suzy nitpicked around the table.

"Oh, I forgot to put out salt and pepper shakers. Silly me!" She ran back and forth to the kitchen several times, coming back with things no one asked for, like a side dish of pickles or extra napkins. She couldn't seem to settle down.

Spice ignored her, accustomed to her mother's insistence on perfection. George looked around nervously. Not much of a talker, George found social activity difficult. He preferred to read or examine maps. Sam always saw new maps, National Geographic magazines, or travel brochures stacked around the den.

Travel was a constant subject with the Crawford family, even though they very seldom traveled. Apparently, Spice's paternal grandmother, Kaweah Crawford, longed to travel but never had the opportunity. She passed on her passion to her son and daughter, who lived in Long Beach, on the coast of Mississippi right on the water.

In lieu of traveling, Kaweah collected vacation brochures and planted seeds and bulbs from around the world in her marvelous garden, which sat on six acres behind the Crawford home that they bought from the estate that Kaweah and the grandfather left to Spice's father and his sister. There were also pecan and tung nut trees. Each fall, Spice gathered nuts from the trees, packaged them, and sold them for extra money.

As Suzy bustled around, Ben grew tired of her hovering. He, unlike Miriam, wasn't intimidated by Suzy. He loved eating dinner at their house. She was truly a stellar cook.

"Mmm-mmm. This sure is good salad!" Ben exclaimed. "Why don't you sit down with us and eat?"

Ben glared at Suzy, and she stared back.

"What's the matter?" Ben asked. "You got a bee up yo' butt tonight, Suzy Q?"

Everyone laughed nervously, but Suzy sat down, and the rest of the evening went well.

~

Throughout Sam's formative years in school, none of her classes made much of an impression. She got A's without studying hard, or she settled for a high B because she didn't want to work. She thought that most of her teachers were boring, and she had little interest in what they had to say. Instead, Sam gorged on fashion magazines and move star pulp.

While Samantha was smart enough, she had no patience for studying and took easy classes whenever she had the chance. Once she threw her geometry book across the room when she attempted to study for a test and didn't understand a problem. Her father, a math genius, was no help. Ben could be harsh, judgmental, and condescending. Sam knew if she asked for his help, as she did one night at the kitchen table, he would yell at her that she was "stupid." That night, she rushed to her room and cried. Rather than risk a scene with her dad, she settled for a lower grade of B, rather than an A.

Instead of pursuing algebra, a subject in which she was deficient, Sam chose to take one semester of typing and shorthand and one semester of home economics. She couldn't see a need for typing and couldn't practice it at home, either, because she didn't have a typewriter. Although she quickly learned shorthand, she didn't use it until she became a professor and had to help her secretary take letters for her in shorthand. In home economics, it took her six weeks to make a straight skirt, which fell apart the first time she wore it. For another six weeks, she cooked delicious biscuits every morning and ate them with butter and jelly before the bell rang.

She did take a world history course, which she thought was interesting, studied for it, and made an A. Still, Sam worried that she had no understanding of a historical timeline.

But the worst class of all was her junior English class, in which the main requirements were to memorize and perform a speech from one of Shakespeare's plays and to write a book report on an American novel. Samantha went to the library and chose Nathanial Hawthorne's *The House of Seven Gables* for her report. She couldn't comprehend the language patterns nor the theme. She made an appointment to see the tiny, purple-haired teacher after school to ask for assistance, but all the teacher said was, "You should be ashamed of yourself for not understanding this book. You're old enough to do so."

The teacher had obviously never read the classic herself, nor did she attempt to read even one page of the novel aloud with Sam, who instantly dropped the book back in the library slot and chose something more juvenile.

By the time Sam finished high school, she knew English grammar backward and forward. She could diagram sentences and made A+ grades. Her class did an excessive amount of grammar study, but never put their words into practice by writing. Sam's ACT score in English was so high (nearly perfect) that when she went to college, she was put in a group to take a placement test for advanced English. But Sam never even began the essay test. Each student was required to write an impromptu essay on a current event. When the proctor wrote the topic on the blackboard, Samantha stood up and left the room without bothering to pick up her pen and paper. Sam had never before written an impromptu essay to be analyzed and graded. In fact, she had never been asked to write a single paragraph.

But She Had No One to Tell

Samantha Ann Cook hurried across the pavement in her three-inch pink stilettos, following the rest of her Sunday school class. She marched with purpose, moist hands clutching her black, leather-bound Bible. The book had pages edged in smooth, fine gold. Her fingers sought the inner edges of the book, soothing away nervous tension against its silky grain.

The warm spring morning would turn hot and humid in just a few hours once the afternoon took over in Poplarville, Mississippi. It was 1957. Sam and ten other adolescent Southern Baptist girls were on their way to cross the street from the First Baptist Church on Main Street, to the Pearl County Courthouse directly across the street. Their mission was to witness to the prisoners in the hope they could convert sinners to salvation.

A serious and religious child, though growing a little more rebellious as she settled into puberty, fourteen-year-old Samantha looked forward to sharing her thoughts with the prisoners. They marched across Front Street, Poplarville's main thoroughfare, and continued on to the stately steps of the public building. The courthouse also had side doors, and the back, on "Back Street," was across the street from the hospital. The buildings were so close that hospital staff could hear prisoners shouting through the windows during the sultry spring and summer months.

The girls climbed the white marble steps to the second floor of the county courthouse, where the prisoners were housed. Leading the way was their teacher, a sweet congregant who wanted to do right by the girls she taught. She had announced the previous week that they would go to the county courthouse to meet the prisoners and give testimony as to why they should become Christians.

Sam planned to read John 3:16 to the prisoners:

> *For God so loved the world that He gave His only begotten Son, that whosoever believeth in Him shall not perish but shall have eternal life.*

Upon entering the cell area, they found two Black men, one White man, and one White woman all sharing a single cell. They were in the same dirty, plaster-walled room and all wore the same drab prison garments of black pants and a grayish-white shirt, which probably would have been white if not for filth and age.

The first thing Sam noticed was the stench of urine and sweat, exacerbated by the heat. Part of the smell emanated from the toilet that sat uncovered in the corner of the cell.

Unkempt, imprisoned, and bored, the prisoners seemed a willing audience to the teenage girls' missionary advances.

The girls took a seat near the guard and each took turns speaking while their teacher remained quiet. She wanted the girls to use their own voices during this experience. Sam's nerves kept her eyes aimed straight ahead. She did not look at the prisoners, but instead listened to what the other girls had to say. When it was her turn, Sam recited her verse and told the prisoners how much her spirituality meant to her.

"God gives me strength and hope," she said in a weak voice. Taking a deep breath, she began again more confidently. "I feel safe when I talk to God. I keep a journal about my fears and hopes for the future. I think deeply about how to keep my life on the right path. If you pray to God, He'll forgive you of your sins, and you'll be able to make a better life for yourselves."

One of the Black men raised his hand, and Sam's heart raced. "If we pray, will God forgive us? Will we be forgiven?"

"Oh yes!" Sam felt proud and a bit giddy. She had touched another soul, and she felt wise and benevolent. It was only a short moment, but it was one she always remembered.

~

The following year, however, Samantha had a new teacher at church whose lessons came into sharp contrast with the inclusive messages they shared with the prisoners. Buxom and large-bellied with a chalk-white, powdery face and purple-rinsed hair to cover her aging silver, Minnie Lou Tenderfoot, wife of Christopher Columbus Tenderfoot, had a reputation that preceded her. Although she had no children of her own, she worked with them every day, and her harmful lessons no doubt extended beyond the walls of the church. In addition to teaching Sunday school, Mrs. Tenderfoot served not only as the school librarian, but also and taught Samantha and her classmates English and math.

Sam's first unforgettable encounter with Mrs. Tenderfoot came during junior high math class. The schools in Poplarville didn't have special education, so among Sam's classmates were several mentally challenged students. One boy named Hulon was what Sam and her friends called a "bus boy," meaning he lived somewhere far out in the country and rode in on a yellow school bus. Hulon never talked and never connected with anyone. He was probably autistic.

One day, Mrs. Tenderfoot told the class to open their math books to page eighteen. Hulon merely sat and grinned. Despite her overabundance of white powder, Mrs. Tenderfoot grew red-faced. She raised her voice and threatened, "Hulon, if you don't open your book, I'll hit you!"

Hulon grinned.

Pow! Mrs. Tenderfoot smacked Hulon's cheek hard with her math book.

Hulon opened his book.

The whole class was so scared, no one knew if poor Hulon found the right page.

The impact of Mrs. Tenderfoot's behavior lasted. None of her students ever questioned her again about anything.

~

Every Sunday, Mrs. Tenderfoot held court over her class of teenage girls. At their previous meeting, Mrs. Tenderfoot had announced that she'd be discussing three special topics in the coming weeks. Although typical lessons were from a quarterly scripture pamphlet, the next few Sundays would come directly from Mrs. Tenderfoot's heart, she said.

The girls all knew there would be no actual "discussion." Listening quietly in the corner of the church's basement, the proper Baptist girls had no choice but to sit still while Mrs. Tenderfoot expounded on how the girls could better follow God's will. During those lessons, she recited what most likely were the rules passed on to her by the men in her life—her husband and the church pastor.

Samantha and her classmates, with spiked heels and cinched waists, stared stone-faced as Mrs. Tenderfoot expounded on the topics she would covered in the following three weeks: *Why Christian Girls Don't Smoke*, *Why Christian Girls Don't Dance*, and *Why Christian Girls Don't Cuss*.

Mrs. Tenderfoot's lesson on why Christian girls don't smoke was lost on Sam. She eventually tried smoking, albeit unsuccessfully.

"She can't even smoke!" her friends taunted as she coughed and choked on her first attempt to inhale. It was her first and last cigarette, smoked in the back seat of Spice's car after they'd been swimming at the all-White community pool one afternoon. Her face burned with embarrassment, as the others laughed, though Spice didn't join in. Darla,

Tandra, and Joan were much better smokers. By that time, Sam had forgotten Mrs. Tenderfoot's lesson, as well as the reasons for it.

The second lesson proved even more comical. The following Sunday, Sam and her friends tried not to giggle as Mrs. Tenderfoot bemoaned, "The Lord has just laid it on my heart, ladies, that I shouldn't dance."

That was ridiculous and totally impractical. Moreover, there was no venue in Poplarville, Mississippi, in which Minnie Lou *could* dance. Her corsets were so tight that wiggling and huffing down the aisle at church produced beads of sweat on her brow, melting away portions of her white powder mask.

As Sam listened to the third lecture, however, her boredom turning to sullen, stifled anger. When it came to cussing, Mrs. Tenderfoot had many reasons to oppose it. Chief among them was that the ideal beauty of the town, an older girl named Mary Marie, would never be heard cussing in her lifetime, according to Mrs. Tenderfoot.

"Beautiful women such as Mary Marie are too refined and cultured to allow defiled words to depart their perfect lips," Mrs. Tenderfoot reminded the girls, believing that many of them aspired to be as much like Mary Marie as possible.

The idea that Mary Marie never uttered an obscenity was a myth. During Sam's early teen years, Mrs. Tenderfoot thought Mary Marie wouldn't cuss because she was eighteen and about to go happily to the college of her choice in Texas. But Mary Marie, who was five-years older than Sam, likely uttered plenty of obscenities after her husband left her twice with four children. Her life became hard.

But Mrs. Tenderfoot didn't stop there. "I'll just tell you, girls," she said. "I'll lay it straight. I'll give you the bottom line about why you shouldn't cuss. The reason is that any little *'nigger'* across the tracks can do it. You're higher and better."

As those words came from Mrs. Tenderfoot's flaming

red lips, Sam burned with anger. She knew it was wrong to say things like that. *"Nigger"* was a mean and ugly word, and no one in Sam's home used it.

She sat there, feeling appalled, anxious, and furious. The small amount of respect she had for Mrs. Tenderfoot vanished. They were in church, where all people were supposed to be respected and valued, where all were equal in the eyes of God. Mrs. Tenderfoot was supposed to be setting an example for the teenage girls. But who could Sam tell?

She knew not to mention it at home. Samantha's mother was a passive person. She might have felt angry, but she would probably just tell Samantha to forget it. That was what Miriam did with all the bad things in her life, so why couldn't Sam do the same?

Ben, on the other hand, could be hotheaded and would almost certainly have given Mrs. Tenderfoot a piece of his mind. He was more opinionated and outspoken than most of the congregants at the Baptist church. When the Cooks joined the church, he was denied a deaconship for honestly speaking his belief that one could fall from grace, which was contrary to Baptist doctrine. He'd been offered the treasurer's position instead, since he was an expert with numbers.

Sam knew that if her father spoke his mind to Mrs. Tenderfoot, Sam would be the topic of gossip in the halls of her small-town school. So, Samantha Ann Cook said nothing. Rather than express her anger, she stuffed it inside.

They Saw the Blood

Sixteen-year-old Samantha felt honored to have been chosen as a junior to sing at the senior prom. The evening was cool and clear, perfect April weather in southern Mississippi. Before her date picked her up, she admired herself in the mirror. Feeling grown-up and beautiful in a taffeta net dress with a hoop skirt, she twirled around. She always remembered the beauty of that dress. The color was sublime, a light mint green that reminded her of the frothy sea. Her date, though fun and romantic, was not as memorable as her dress.

Poplarville students finishing their last two years of high school attended classes at the junior college, and their prom was held in the college's gymnasium. On that magical night, Sam sang romantic soprano solos from the '20s, '30s, and '40s with the band from the junior college—"In My Alice Blue Gown," "Some Enchanted Evening," and "I'll Be Seeing You."

But as she sang her songs at her Whites-only school, a Black man was being tortured in the most vile manner at the courthouse across town. He would be murdered later that night, shot, weighted down, and dumped over a bridge into the Pearl River, which runs along the border between Mississippi and Louisiana, between Poplarville and Bogalusa.

It was a bridge many teens from Sam's hometown

were familiar with because they crossed it regularly as they traveled the twenty miles to Bogalusa, Louisiana, to drink alcohol legally. Poplarville, like all of Pearl River County, was dry. The Baptist vote ensured that the county maintained its dry status at every election. But there was no legal drinking age, so outside the county, teens could acquire alcohol as easily as an adult wherever it was sold.

Sam and Spice, along with their dates, were out until three o'clock that morning, though they had turned down invitations to go drink liquor in Gulfport or Bogalusa. After the prom, Sam and six of her friends went to another girl's house for breakfast. Sam barely knew the girl, who was a year or two younger, but her mother, probably aware of Sam's reputation as a good girl, may have been trying to keep her daughter out of trouble that night. She likely called Miriam to ask if Sam and her friends could come to their house after prom.

The girls, their boyfriends, and a few other couples went to the girl's house for breakfast around one in the morning. They ate a bountiful feast of eggs, biscuits, bacon, and soft drinks. After a fun time chatting and laughing, excited about being out so late, they headed home around three o'clock.

The following morning, Samantha was awakened by a call from Spice, who had double-dated with her. She looked at the clock and saw that it was ten o'clock.

"A man was killed last night at the courthouse," Spice said urgently. "They say the blood is still there. Let's go. I'll pick you up."

Sam was never able to remember afterward if she or Spice told their parents where they went, or if they talked to them about what they saw at the courthouse when they returned home. It was a Saturday, so both their fathers were home.

Sam and Spice arrived at the courthouse that morning to find a crowd of about a hundred people milling around. In hindsight, Sam realized they were all White. At the time, though, that didn't even register. Poplarville's Black population was invisible to the White population, and she wasn't accustomed to mingling with anyone other than Whites.

Although it had been hours since the crime was committed, there was no police tape marking off the scene. Residents viewed the spectacle with interest and curiosity, not taking any care to avoid contaminating the area.

Sam and Spice entered through the side door of the old courthouse and walked up the steps to the building's second floor. They stepped around thick trails of blood on the white, worn, marble steps they'd climbed many times before. Sam had walked those stairs when she'd witnessed to the prisoners several years prior and when her middle school civics class had visited the courtroom to witness a real trial that lasted over a month. In another town just south of theirs, a White man had killed his own brother. The jury declared the him guilty of murder in the first degree, but the judge ruled against punishing the perpetrator. He received no sentence of any kind.

"How can that be?" Samantha asked the teacher when they were back in class. "Our book says everyone who's convicted by a jury gets punishment. This man got none."

Her teacher didn't reply. Instead, he pretended he hadn't heard the question.

Though the courthouse steps were familiar, they now felt foreign and scary. When Sam and Spice reached the second floor, they saw pools of blood spattered on the landing in front of the cells, where frightened prisoners remained. They had witnessed what was clearly a foul and frightful nighttime event.

Sam and Spice had no knowledge of Mack Charles Parker or the crime of rape he allegedly committed. They were only teenage girls, and no one spoke of such things to them. But as with most lynchings, this premeditated murder occurred with the knowledge of many of the White adults in town.

The townspeople of Poplarville eventually learned

the gist of what happened, or at least the White version of the story. Between town gossip, the FBI investigation, and probing from the three major TV outlets that set up shop in Poplarville for several months (NBC, ABC, and CBS), Sam pieced together the basic story, but it took years to sort truth from rumor. Newspaper articles, a book, and Internet research, including the original FBI files, were eventually made available for those interested in parsing the whole story, which included Sam.

The events that led to Parker's demise began on February 23, 1958, as a young married couple, Jimmy and June Walters, along with their small daughter, were driving north from New Orleans on the old two-lane Route 11 that ran from New Orleans to New York, the only highway then available for traveling between the two cities. The family intended to drive along the short stretch from Bogalusa, where they had been visiting family, to their home north in Petal just outside Hattiesburg. They had to turn onto Highway 11 in Poplarville. The next town would be Lumberton.

Around midnight on that February night, their car broke down from lack of gasoline south of Lumberton but within Pearl River County, where Poplarville was the county seat. Jimmy Walters knew the area well enough to know there would be no traffic along that highway during such a late hour. Besides, the weather had begun to sleet, and June was pregnant. Their four-year-old daughter, Debbie Carol, was barely awake. Jimmy believed he had no choice but to make the trek into Lumberton to try to get help.

Supposedly, Mack Charles Parker and four of his friends happened by soon after Jimmy left his wife with instructions to lock the car and open it for no one. Upon seeing the car, Parker slowed, thinking he would check to see if the tires were worth stealing. He stopped to peer into the window. Once he realized people were inside, he and his friends left. The local story goes that he returned from Lumberton alone and raped June Walters in the presence of her child.

Parker was arrested, and June identified him in a police lineup.

There was much more to the story, but those were the basic claims of what supposedly happened that evening. Arguments arose that cast doubt on Parker's guilt. Since his trial would never come into play, only gossip and speculation were available. In February, Parker was indicted on one count of rape and two counts of kidnapping and was transferred to the Pearl River County Courthouse in Poplarville. Parker vociferously pleaded not guilty to all charges but never had a chance to attest his innocence because he was murdered three days before the trial was to begin on Monday morning.

Two men in particular, former Deputy Sheriff J. P. Walker and James Floren Lee, an itinerant preacher, incited and organized the lynch mob that dragged Parker from his cell. They used the swirl of rumors, fear of Northerners, and anger against Blacks who stepped out of line.

J. P. Walker had made it known that he would run for sheriff again when the current Sheriff Osborn Moody named his successor. He maintained his status as a politician and made it his business to know what was going on in his precinct. Thinking to use the Parker case to garner votes, he headed out one April evening to Gumpond, Mississippi, six miles east of Poplarville.

On a Wednesday night at Preacher Lee's Baptist congregation, and Walker knew he could count on Lee to incite the crowd to racially charged hysteria. After the sermon, Walker met with Preacher Lee, two other friends, and Preacher Lee's son Jeff. Together, the five men decided they would ensure Parker never had a trial.

The next day, the five men gathered a crowd of thirty from the surrounding areas, including Gumpond, Hattiesburg, McNeil, Picayune, Poplarville, and Lumberton. Jeff Lee and another man went to Jimmy Walters, trying unsuccessfully to persuade him to help, but Walters flatly refused.

Jimmy and June Walters were very vocal about their position against violence toward Parker. June wasn't entirely sure that Parker was the man who raped her. But it was too late. Both Jimmy and June became the focus of public scorn and ridicule for not taking steps toward revenge against Parker. The case became solely about race. It was no longer in the interest of justice for June. The Parker case was doomed to be a vicious "lesson" for the people of color in Pearl River County.

Unlike Emmett Till, who was perversely attacked and gruesomely murdered in northern Mississippi a few years earlier without even being arrested, Mack Charles Parker was slated for a court date the following Monday. He awaited trial in the local jail when a few men climbed the worn, white marble steps to the jail cell on the third floor. Ten men, who had agreed to draw lots as to who would go, and the other men of the mob would never know who actually went. The men did not even have to break in. They gained access with a key that was left on the deputy sheriff's desk in his office on the first floor. It was rumored that his window just happened to be left open on that cool, brisk evening and the key placed there with the express purpose of allowing the mob entrance to the courthouse. In some versions of the story, the deputy sheriff accompanied the mob.

Once inside, the men beat Parker and gruesomely castrated him. (Later, the one woman prisoner who witnessed it took her own life, as did one of the perpetrators.) They dragged him by his feet, his head bumping all the way down three flights of marble stairs, out of the courthouse, and into a car headed twenty miles west to the Pearl River.

The red blood was left on the old worn white marble steps for the whole world, including Sam and Spice, to see the next morning. When the murderers arrived at the Pearl River Bridge, they made sure the roads were clear, pulled Parker from the car, and shot him in the chest at close range. They weighted him down with logging chains and threw his body into the churning, fast-flowing water.

The Aftermath

Not since Emmett Till's lynching had there been such a media outcry. Mack Charles Parker's murder would eventually be described as "one of the last lynchings in America" by author and historian Howard Smead in his book *Blood Justice: The Lynching of Mack Charles Parker*. Although lynchings typically generate images of hanging, they were in fact often murder by other means, such as burning at the stake, dismemberment, or gunshot. According to Smead, Mack Charles Parker's lynching "carried many of the notorious elements of past Southern lynchings: charges of interracial rape, a mob storming the jail, widespread and detailed knowledge of the lynching conspiracy before and after, and no punishment for the mob."

The day after Parker's death, the news was reported as far as Paris and Moscow. In Poplarville, rumors swirled, yet the episode never even made it into the town's local paper, *The Democrat*. The irony of *The Democrat*'s silence didn't escape Sam later in life. Most White Southerners, Democrat or Republican, were segregationists, including Samantha's parents. In small Southern towns, views tended toward the conservative side no matter which party one voted for.

Race was a powerful motivator in elections, and both parties used racism to rally voters. The National Association for the Advancement of Colored People (NAACP) was viewed by Whites with great suspicion, many of these Whites claimed that the group was a communist front organization.

Subsequent to the lynching, the FBI was ordered into Poplarville at dawn by President Eisenhower after the sheriff finally called Governor Coleman. They stayed for three months and interviewed nearly every resident of Poplarville. They even questioned Samantha twice in her family's living room.

"Did you hear any talk in town about this event beforehand?" the agents asked teenage Sam.

"No, Sir."

"Did you know this man was in jail or what he was there for?"

"No."

"Did you see or hear anything unusual that night?"

"No. I was dancing and singing at the prom."

"Where did you go afterward?"

"To a friend's house on North Street. Her mother cooked breakfast for us."

"When did you first learn about this event?"

"When my friend Spice called me and woke me up at ten o'clock that morning. She said she heard about the murder, the lynching, and that blood was still on the courthouse steps."

"Did you go?"

"Yes. We went in her car."

"What did you see when you arrived?"

"The scene wasn't roped off yet. There was no yellow tape. Crowds gathered around. There was blood on the sidewalk and outside on the street. Fresh blood was on each courthouse step. We walked all the way up to the jail. There was blood on all the white marble."

"Did you know of any other young people who went to the prom but went out of town afterward?"

"Yes. I know some who went to the Mississippi Coast, to Gulfport or Biloxi, and some who went to Bogalusa,

Louisiana, to drink liquor. Our town doesn't sell it."

"Have you talked to them?"

"Yes."

"Did they see anything unusual?"

"Some did. The ones who went to Bogalusa saw something large being thrown off the Pearl River Bridge on the south side from a stopped car. Strange men were throwing something off, something big, probably wrapped in a burlap bag."

"Would you tell us the names of those friends who told you this?"

"Yes," answered Samantha. And she did.

Sam didn't know if the rumor of her friends having seen a body inside of a bag being thrown from the bridge was true, but she later learned that Mack Charles Parker's body had, indeed, been found in the river.

~

On a sweltering Sunday morning, Samantha, Lilah Jo, and their parents parked down the street and walked several blocks to church because the church's parking lot was filled with media vans from the country's major news stations. The media had been there for months, taking up space in the church parking lot while FBI men in their dark suits and straw fedoras crowded the streets.

It was strange, with all the goings-on about town, that no one talked about why the FBI was there. Everyone pretended they knew nothing, including their preacher. His sermon that week was about persecution.

"This business is tearing our town apart," he began that morning. "Northern agitators have come to our small town. We're good people," he stressed throughout his sermon. "They" were evil. He claimed the Northerners who came to town were there to ruin the townsfolk's peaceful lives.

Samantha stared out the window at the street that joined their church and the courthouse, remembering the pools of blood. No one from her town had been arrested or charged. One man was dead by his own gun. Everybody believed he had been a part of committing this atrocity, yet it was not proven since he never went to trial. It seemed like the Poplarville government had blood on its hands. How could a man possibly be abducted from the courthouse without witnesses? How had they gained entrance to the building?

As Sam listened to her preacher, a seemingly good, educated, intelligent man, defend their town instead of talking about the injustice that occurred, she felt a bitter disgust in her stomach.

After Sunday school with Mrs. Tenderfoot, Samantha waited for her parents and sister to meet her outside the church to walk down the street to their car. She saw the preacher come outside, offering his wide, toothy smile. He cozied up to the men in the media vans, constantly smiling, as he chatted with them for a few moments. Pointing to the street, he added a few more words. A short time later, Samantha watched all the vans slowly depart the parking lot.

Sam again felt disgusted. Poplarville wouldn't even open its parking lots to the media, who only sought the truth. Her preacher had never once mentioned the lynching in his sermon that morning, nor on any other Sunday morning. Her preacher, a man of God, was covering his eyes.

There were certain things that the polite White citizens of Poplarville never discussed, even when those things stared them in the face. Many years after the Parker lynching, when the local pool was filled in and the Poplarville school was finally integrated, no one talked about it. Around the same time, when the community center across the street from where Sam's family lived was torn down. No one explained why.

After the preacher had banished the media vans from the church parking lot, they began parking on the street beside the courthouse. That delayed traffic even more and further irritated Poplarville's twelve hundred or so residents.

Meanwhile, the local paper continued its silence, but much later Sam learned that other small-town newspapers covered the story. The editorials in *The Democrat,* the local Poplarville paper, wrote only that their town was a good one, filled with good people from the good state of Mississippi, and that the rest of the country should let them be. However, by the following day, papers in London, Paris, Moscow and New York were covering the story. Although lynchings had been prevalent throughout the South, this was the first to receive major international publicity since that of Emit Till, presumably due to the FBI.

Without proper local media coverage, the townspeople only had rumors to go on. It got around town that the mother of Mr. Parker, who was from Lumberton, hired an NAACP lawyer from Chicago. That lawyer, if he were allowed the chance to defend Parker, was going to "git the bastard off scot-free." The lawyer would supposedly be able to do that even with the local all-White, all-male jury and the notorious old White male judge, Sebe Dale.

Prior to Parker's murder, the growing concern among locals was that even if Parker were convicted in Poplarville, his case would go to an appeals court, where the charges would be dropped, or he would receive a lighter sentence.

Those suspicions and fears in the masses with talk of the NAACP weren't based on truth. Parker's mother had hired a Black trial lawyer, but the NAACP wasn't involved in the hiring. Yet none of those factual details mattered to the White townspeople of Poplarville.

~

Benjamin Warren Cook, though not a politically liberal man, was fair-minded with strong opinions that sometimes got him into trouble. He told Sam several times that he would never serve on a jury in their town. He said all the judges were crooked, that if he voted with his conscience, he might find his business blown up. Samantha hadn't believed him at the time.

When the FBI came to town in response to the Parker

murder, Sam's dad was fascinated. Being a numbers man, he understood the importance of examining minute details. He appreciated the tedious, patient manner with which the FBI questioned the entire town.

Poplarville was a small community with little real estate available to rent for such a sudden explosion in workers. Between the federal law enforcement agents and the media, the town was bursting at the seams. The streets were crowded. The few cafes had long lines for lunch each day. The FBI rented a tiny office over a law firm across the street from Ben's auto dealership. It was probably the only place they could get, either for lack of space or lack of hospitality.

As Ben left for lunch one day, he decided to go to the FBI office to welcome the investigators to town. He was a Christian man, and he wanted them to know there were some in town who appreciated the work they were doing. Given to spontaneity, he was always ready for new ideas.

Ben went upstairs in the office building across the street. Hearing multiple typewriters clicking and dinging, he peeked in. Officers were jammed into the tiny room, spilling all over each other, trying to type reports and examine their interview notes. It was blazing hot in the room. All of the FBI men were drenched in sweat.

"Hello, Boys," Ben called into the room.

Several sweaty men peered up at him. Ben, a short man with balding hair, was not an imposing figure. As a salesman, he always smiled cheerfully when he was in public.

"Hello, Sir," one man replied wearily.

A couple more stared suspiciously. They hadn't been given a very warm welcome by most of the townspeople.

"I just wanted to come over to introduce myself. I'm Ben Cook. That's my dealership across the street, Cook Ford Company. I'd like to welcome you to town."

The men smiled a bit more cheerfully than when they initially saw him. He stayed a while to chitchat. As they talked, some of the men complained about their cramped quarters. Ben's offices at the dealership were always empty at noon, and he had an idea.

"Every day we clear out for lunch at noon," Ben said. "Would y'all like to use our three vacant and air-conditioned offices for that hour each day? You'd be able to spread out easily and type your reports in the cool."

A man who sat nearby and listened to Ben share his hospitable plan suddenly stood, smiled, and slapped Ben's back. "That sounds fantastic, friend."

Every day for three weeks, several of the FBI men headed to the dealership at noon to enjoy some legroom and air-conditioning, which their rented office across the street didn't have.

Three weeks into the arrangement, Ben was sitting in his office when his private line rang. Expecting his wife or a friend, he heard an unknown man's voice on the other end.

"If you don't get those SOBs out of your building, we's ready to blow it up."

The line went dead.

Ben's first thought was his family. He had to make a living. He knew Miriam, Sam, and Lilah Jo would be in danger if he kept helping the FBI. He needed his business to put his daughters through college. His employees might be in danger, too. Besides, he hadn't even paid for the car dealership yet.

Ben walked quickly across the street and told the FBI men what happened. He asked them, please, for his safety's sake, not to come back.

That evening when Ben came home, he was more stressed than usual. Miriam knew something was wrong and atypically asked, "What's wrong, Ben?"

He sat at the kitchen table, peering into the living room, where his daughters did their homework. "I'll tell you later."

That evening in bed, Ben confided the story to Miriam.

Her eyes widened in fear. "My goodness, Ben" she whispered, "What if they blow up the building? What'll we do? Should we tell the police?"

He shook his head. "It's been taken care of. The FBI

won't come back."

Miriam, though terrified, kept quiet. It was one of those moments when she knew it was better not to argue with her husband. His fear was too great. Both were silent, lost in thoughts that were too unnerving to discuss. Settling down under the covers, Miriam silently turned off the bedside lamp. They turned their backs to each other and lay silently in the dark.

Neither of them mentioned the incident again until several years later. Sam heard the story from her father shortly before he died, when she was twenty-one and Ben was forty-seven. Ben's heart problems had begun while Sam was still in high school. During those years, he was in constant pain with angina. Like Sam's brother, who died from heart failure soon after birth, Ben's heart troubles began a few years before the proper surgery would become available to extend his life. By the time the life-saving surgery was available, it was too late.

A few years prior to Ben's death, Sam spent a lot of time with him one summer during college, when she took classes at the local community college. During those three months, Sam attended classes for four hours each morning, came home for lunch, and spent her afternoons downtown, working for Ben at the auto dealership. Working for him was just a pretext to spend time with him, because she knew he would die. And she was right—he was dead within one year.

When Ben was near to passing, he sat down with Sam one evening when she was visiting from college in Texas.

"Sam, come here," he called from the living room.

Sam sat on the couch beside him. She felt a special tenderness toward him in those days. He didn't look good. Most of his hair was gone, and what was left seemed gray and lifeless, settled atop his worn skin. He breathed heavily, as he always did in those days. Ben wanted to tell Sam about his attempts to help the FBI and the threatening phone call he received. He knew he had little time left to impart any wisdom to his daughter, and he hoped that she would understand.

As he recounted the story, Sam's juvenile arrogance kicked in and all of the softness she felt for her sick father quickly faded away.

"You were a coward!" she said.

"No," he said sternly. "I wasn't. I had to keep my car dealership. I needed to make our living. I had to send you and your sister to college, where I never got to go." Ben sighed, wondering if he did the right thing by telling her about something that happened five years prior.

By the time Samantha understood his position, it was too late. He was dead. She would always regret the words she said to her father in his last days.

Years later, after Miriam developed dementia and was moved to an assisted-living home, Sam was staying in her mother's house alone when the son of Joe, one of Ben's former employees, came to see her. It had been many years since Ben died.

Old Joe's son told Sam his memories of Mr. Ben's Easter egg roll for the Black employees' children. One spring, Ben had held a second Easter Egg Roll in their backyard the week after he held one for the White kids. He grilled hamburgers, just as he did the previous week. Sam remembered it all. Joe's son told Sam he never, before or since, knew such a kind White man. He also told Sam that his father, Old Joe, sadly took his own life.

~

The Mack Charles Parker lynching was an event that still cannot be discussed with many of Samantha's hometown friends. Most people from Poplarville saw only a villain in Mark Charles Parker and saw what happened to him as acceptable vigilante justice.

Many citizens of Poplarville, especially the most prominent members of the town, never admitted or spoke publicly about the racially charged violence that churned beneath the surface of their community. Those who did speak up said that the FBI eventually learned the truth, including the names of the murderers.

In all the months the FBI worked in the town, they couldn't prove the case was a federal one. At the time, to be considered a federal case, the perpetrators had to have crossed state lines. It was never proven whether the mob threw Parker into the river on the Mississippi side or the Louisiana side of the bridge.

After several months, the FBI turned its research and evidence over to the Mississippi Grand Jury. No one was ever indicted, much less tried, for Parker's murder.

Where Does She Go from Here?

During her senior year of high school, Sam gave up the jitterbug at the Friday night dances, as well as her role as a majorette in the String of Pearls for the junior college band. She did it all for Jesus. Their preacher spoke against dancing and wearing revealing clothing. The String of Pearls members were getting new outfits, and they were too short. There were also leotards, which were too revealing. Sam wanted to remain pure.

She figured she might become a Baptist missionary, ministering to the poor in some faraway country. She always imagined it would be hot. Maybe she'd go to Africa. The poor souls were probably going to hell.

She would decide about her future in college, she thought, but first, she wanted to become completely educated, which she realized wouldn't happen in Poplarville. She told Bobby, when she met him one day in Birmingham, that she wanted to know how things got the way they were. She supposed she might major in history. He told her he had no interest in that subject, nor in anything but the present.

Samantha graduated from high school with honors, the fourth-highest graduate in her tiny class of thirty-two students. Their graduation ceremony was held on a raised stage on the Pearl River Junior College football field, with an audience of family and friends cheering from the bleachers. It was a cold spring day, and they wore heavy coats to graduation practice.

Freezing or not, all the girls in the class wore new summer dresses under their gowns. Sam's was homemade by Miriam. The dress had a pink organdy full-gathered skirt trimmed in white lace. Sam wore white, spiked summer high heels. A memory of the dress and the moment was captured in a photograph of Sam receiving her diploma and shaking hands with Mr. Garvin Johnston, the diploma presenter and president of the two-year college.

Nothing had been decided about where Sam would go to college. Most of the college-bound students in her class planned to attend Pearl River College for two years before transferring somewhere else, such as Mississippi State or Ole Miss. Ben tried to convince Sam to do the same, choosing one or two future professions for her.

Either she could stay in town and get a job in a beauty shop, which required the study of cosmetology, or she could study medical technology for a job at the local hospital, working seven to three. As he put it, she'd "be home by the time her children got home."

But Sam had other plans. Not only did she want to go out of state, but she insisted on attending a Baptist college or university. She visited Mississippi College in Clinton and Stanford University, the Baptist college in Alabama. Both were too narrow and fundamentalist for Sam. She didn't feel comfortable with the strict atmosphere and rigid rules. These colleges began every class with prayer, which, though she was religious, turned Sam off. She thought that education should be separate from religion.

The summer after her junior year in high school, Samantha had worked at Glorieta Baptist Assembly outside Santa Fe, New Mexico, for six weeks. The popular encampment hosted retreats, conferences, and camps for all ages throughout the summer. To get the job, she pretended to be a year older than she was. While there, she met many college students working on the Glorieta staff who were students at Baylor University in Waco, Texas. They all loved Baylor and advised Sam to go there if she possibly could.

Baylor's tuition was expensive, especially for the time. Samantha knew her dad would fight the idea on several grounds — it cost too much, and it was too far from home. She could more easily stay home and attend the community college or the Baptist school, Mississippi College, in Clinton, Mississippi.

But Sam set her heart on attending Baylor University in Waco, a place she'd never seen. She would go there or not at all. She and her dad didn't speak about it. High school graduation came and went, and another week passed without discussing the matter. About seven days after graduation, Ben came home and announced that he'd telephoned Baylor, and they accepted Sam's ACT test scores, which meant she could enroll immediately. He had already made her first tuition payment.

Samantha Ann Cook left Mississippi in late August of that year. With Ben driving and Sam and Miriam both in the front seat of a Lincoln Continental borrowed from Ben's mentor, J. O. Barron in Hattiesburg, they drove away from Poplarville. Ben had the back seat removed to accommodate Sam's clothes and her seventeen hatboxes. Hats were always required for Baylor girls to wear to church, but by the time Sam arrived on campus in the fall of 1960, the university dropped the rule. Sam never wore even one of those hats.

Also, just two months before she graduated from college, Ben died. By the time she finished her education many years later, Sam had acquired four degrees: one in history, two in English, and one in education — the last so she could teach school and earn a living if it became necessary. And it did turn out to be necessary. Sam eventually became a university professor.

Conclusion

When Samantha left for college, she finally felt free to learn, to express her own opinions, and to discover who she truly was and wanted to be. She was now free to acknowledge realities of Mississippi culture that she previously never admitted.

For Sam, an underlying nostalgic pull is strong and present even now concerning her Mississippi background. Memories abound in her heart and mind as she looks to the past, the images flashing before her like the landscapes out windows of the fast-moving trains of her childhood.

Who would ever be as kind and generous to her as Mrs. Grace, a Southern lady who kept her for two weeks and bought her a beautiful red dress with matching shoes, socks, and purse to help her feel special when her sister was born? Who but her father, Ben Cook, would haul a boat all the way to Destin just so Sam could go waterskiing with her best friend? Who but Audri Goodrich would ever comb her hair every morning for six weeks before school because Sam's mom had gone far away to see her own dying mother? Who else but Mamaw Lola would hand stitch quilts for Sam's dolls, or make delicious feasts of fried chicken, pickled vegetables, and sweet tea for her? Would Sam ever again meet such a cast of characters, friends, and teachers? These people shaped her life, and without them she would not be the woman she is today.

But Sam is also free to admit that the time and place of her childhood, with all of the kindness she experienced, was also rife with prejudice and racial violence. Concerning her enlightened beliefs about justice, racism, and hate, few in her community had her back.

Samantha Ann Cook was both found and lost in Mississippi.

Acknowledgments

I must thank several people who helped me immeasurably with this manuscript. First, Martha Wood of Austin, TX, a ghostwriter, was invaluable. For one year, I wrote my memories and episodes of my childhood to her via email. She wrote back after a week, asking questions and instructing me how to flesh out the material. Often, she did it herself, always asking if she was "onto it" and correct. A few times, I had to explain older terminology she hadn't heard before, as Martha is a good deal younger than I.

Katherine Don of Yellow Bird Editors read the manuscript and changed it a good deal. I secured the names of both Martha and Katherine from the Austin Writers' League

My sister, Cheryl Roemmele, read it and offered comments and corrections.

Finally, thanks to the Alamo Bay Press team: Lowell Mick White, Pamela Booton and Diane Wilson.

Without these people and their work and encouragement, I could not have written this book. Thank you all, but I'm especially indebted to Pam for her "onward" attitude and for reminding me why she thought it was important to complete this work—because I was witness to an era, a geography, and a culture that most people do not know.

Finally, I thank my dear husband Ted for all his support and his computer skills.

About Sybil Pittman Estess

Sybil Arlene Pittman Estess was born and raised in Mississippi, which is the subject of this book. She attended Baylor University, where she met her husband, Ted L. Estess. From 1964 to 1965, Sybil taught middle school in her hometown of Poplarville. She speaks of it as one of the most difficult years of her life. She knew only one other woman under thirty years old in the town of fifteen hundred people, and at that time, integration and civil rights still had not begun in that part of Mississippi.

She witnessed Ku Klux Klan rallies and parades. She experienced the lynching of Mack Charles Parker in the courthouse across from the Baptist church in her hometown on Front Street. Seven years later, she watched Martin Luther King's "I Have a Dream" speech at the side of her dying father. They sat on a couch together when she was home from college and he was home from work, too ill to go even to downtown from their home.

In 1965, she and many others suffered the loss of a friend in Vietnam. He was among the first war casualties. Sybil's widowed mother married the young man's widowed father, and no one in either family ever recovered from that senseless death.

Sybil married in 1966 and lived in Louisville, Kentucky, until 1968, when she completed her master's degree in English from the University of Kentucky in Lexington. In 1968, she and Ted moved to Syracuse, New York, for him to attend graduate school. Staying in upstate New York longer than they had planned, Sybil finished her PhD at Syracuse University in 1976. In 1977, the couple moved to Houston, where they have lived for forty years.

Sybil has eight other published books, including five poetry books, an edited collection of essays on Elizabeth Bishop, and a coauthored creative writing text. She has been nominated three times for Poet Laureate of Texas and was a finalist in 2009.

Mississippi Milkwater is Sybil Estess's first book-length work of personal prose.